FROM CHIMPS

TO HUMANS?

CHAPTER 1
Whose Origin of Species?

CHAPTER 2
Is this evolution?

CHAPTER 3
Whose Footprints?

CHAPTER 4
Lucy Who?

CHAPTER 5
Mr. 1470

CHAPTER 6
Four Homos to go

CHAPTER 7
Brains

CHAPTER 8
2003

CHAPTER 9
The Gap

CHAPTER 10
Ice Age or Global Warming?

CHAPTER 11
Changing the Cereals

CHAPTER 12
Where did civilization come from?

CHAPTER 13
King Lists and God Lists

CHAPTER 14
The Ancient Written Record

CHAPTER 1

Whose Origin of Species?

Before the time of Darwin, just under 200 years ago, conventional wisdom had it that God created Adam and Eve and this was the beginning for us humans. That's what Albrecht Durer engraved in about 1500 AD., complete with modest fig leaves and Eve tempting Adam with an apple:

But, famous artist though he was, they both have navels. Navels are where the mother and child are connected by an umbilical cord until the birth of the child. If God created them, they would not have had navels. In the time of Durer in the Western World the church discouraged people from thinking too clearly about the stories in the Bible, either by burning them alive at the stake or stretching them on the rack as heretics. But Columbus had already reached the new world, Martin Luther was alive and well, peasants were rebelling in Europe, and the hold of the church on men's minds was slipping.

After the protestant reformation people had more freedom to question things. It gradually became apparent that the world was far older than the 6000 or so years you get by adding up the dates in the Bible from Adam to the present:

And Adam lived an hundred and thirty years, and begat a son in his own likeness, after his image; and called his name Seth:

And the days of Adam after he had begotten Seth were eight hundred years: and he begat sons and daughters:

And all the days that Adam lived were nine hundred and thirty years: and he died.

And Seth lived an hundred and five years, and begat Enos:

And Seth lived after he begat Enos eight hundred and seven years, and begat sons and daughters:

And all the days of Seth were nine hundred and twelve years: and he died.

And Enos lived ninety years, and begat Cainan:

And so on down to Abraham and then Moses.

By the early 19th century, specimen hunters were collecting samples of all kinds of living creatures from around the world, selling live ones to European zoos, and dead ones to museums. One of these specimen hunters was the Englishman Alfred Wallace. His father had been a librarian. Young Wallace developed an intense interest in "natural history". He was a voracious reader. He met Henry Walter Bates, an avid collector of beetles. In 1845 Wallace told Bates about an exciting new book called Vestiges of the Natural History of Creation. That book contained the hypothesis that there was a natural law by which a simpler life form gave birth to the type next above it and so on to the highest, with each advance being very small.

That there is "a progress of some kind" was supported by the fossil hunters, but still denied by orthodox geologists such as the famous Sir Charles Lyell. Lyell was known to Charles Darwin. Darwin had written a book called the "Journal". Wallace read Darwin's book in 1842-3. Darwin was somewhat long-winded, and so the full title was:

Journal of Researches Into the Geology and Natural History of the Various Countries Visited by H.M.S. Beagle Under the Command of Captain Fitzroy, R.N. From 1832-1836 (published in 1839)

Captain Fitzroy had given Darwin a copy of the first volume of Lyell's Principles (on Geology) at the start of the voyage. This was the voyage during which Darwin studied the finches and other life on the Galapagos Islands near South America. But even in the last edition Darwin said nothing of evolution.

In 1847 Wallace and Bates discussed a trip to the tropics to collect specimens, and later that year Wallace wrote to Bates:

I begin to feel rather dissatisfied with a mere local collection....I should like to take some one family to study thoroughly, principally with a view to the theory of the origin of species

Wallace proposed a joint expedition to the river Amazon. They were assured by a Mr. Doubleday of the British Museum that by collecting insects, birds, mammals and snails, they should be able to cover expenses.

After this trip Wallace went to the New Guinea area and here history was made. In February of 1858 he was at Ternate, one of the Moluccas Islands west of New Guinea east of Borneo and South of the Phillippines. There he had a flash of insight, thought it out in a few hours and wrote it down with a sketch of its various applications, copied it on to letter paper and sent it

off to Charles Darwin, all within a week. The whole paper was about ten pages long He called it

On the Tendency of Varieties To Depart Indefinitely From the Original Type.

Here is the gist of his argument, mostly in his own words:

1. Domesticated animals, if left to themselves, tend to return to their wild type. This has led orthodox naturalists to a somewhat prejudiced belief in the stability of species.

2. This assumption is altogether false. There is a general principle in nature causing many varieties to survive the parent species and to give rise to successive variations further and further from the original type.

3. The life of wild animals is a struggle for existence. It requires the full exertion of all their faculties and energies to preserve their own existence and provide for their infant offspring.

4. Large animals cannot be so abundant as small ones. Lions can never be as plentiful as antelopes. The greater or less fecundity of an animal is often considered to be one of the chief causes of its abundance or scarcity: but consideration of the facts will show us it really has little or nothing to do with

the matter. Even the least prolific of animals would increase rapidly if unchecked, whereas it is evident that the animal population of the globe must be stationary or perhaps through the influence of man, decreasing. Very few birds produce less than two young ones each year. Four will certainly be below average. If we suppose that each pair produce young only four times in their life (also below average)....a simple calculation will show that in 15 years each pair of birds would have increased to nearly 10 million, whereas we have no reason to believe that the number of birds ....increases at all in 15 or 150 years.

5. It would therefore appear that as far as the continuance of the species and the keeping up of the average number of individuals are concerned, large broods are superfluous.

6. It is evident therefore that each year an immense number of birds must perish--as many in fact as are born. It follows that whatever the average existing number, twice that number must perish annually.

7. Now it is clear that what takes place among the individuals of a species must also occur among the several allied species of a group..viz. that those which are best adapted to obtain a regular supply of food and to defend themselves against enemies and climate must necessarily obtain and preserve a superiority in population.

8. Most or perhaps all variations from the typical form of a species must have some definite effect, however slight, on habits or capabilities--even a change in colour might affect their safety.

9. Now let some alteration of physical conditions occur -- drought, or a locust plague -- say this takes the utmost powers to avoid a complete extermination; the most feebly organized soon become extinct. The superior variety would then alone remain, and on return to favourable circumstances rapidly increase in numbers.
10. The variety would now have replaced the species of which it would be a more perfectly developed and more highly organized form. Such a variety could not return to its original form, for that form is inferior and could never compete with it for existence.

11. This progression of certain varieties by minute steps is a tendency in nature to which there appears no reason to assign any definite limits.

This brilliant paper hit Charles Darwin like an exploding bomb. It had been twenty years since his studies and notes on the Galapagos Islands. All this time he had spent laboriously considering the problem of evolution but it seems to me he had never been able to figure out how it might work. Now this young unknown had dashed off a paper in a few hours of intuitive insight and given him the key to the problem. There was considerable class snobbery in Victorian England and collectors such as Alfred Wallace were looked down upon by the natural scientists. Charles Darwin mingled with the scientists. He had originally studied theology at Cambridge. His grandfather, Dr. Erasmus Darwin, was a member of the prestigious and scholarly Linnean Society. Sir Charles Lyell was the leading geologist of his time and Sir Joseph Hooker was the most eminent biologist. Both were intimate friends of Charles Darwin. All three were members of the Linnean Society, Charles Darwin being admitted in 1854.

Charles Darwin had married his cousin, a member of the wealthy Wedgwood family, of pottery fame. He had written and published extensively on various topics in natural history. He spent ten years studying barnacles and many more on pigeons. As to his great book on evolution, in December of 1857 Darwin wrote:

My work on which I have now been at work more or less for 20 years, will not fix or settle anything; but I hope it will aid by giving a large collection of facts.....
Darwin told Lyell about his shock at receiving Wallace's paper. Lyell told Darwin to leave it to him and to Hooker to deal with.

What Lyell and Hooker did was arrange a special meeting of the Linnean Society for July 1, 1858, at which two unpublished pieces by Darwin were read first, touching on evolutionary matters, followed by a reading of Wallace's paper. It is questionable whether or not the excerpts from Darwin were written after he received Wallace's paper.

Personally, in my reading of Darwin's "Origin", I found him to be a rather verbose writer. By page 19 he had already listed the same variety of dog breeds three times. His work is poorly referenced. On one page (17) he says:

Horner's researches have rendered it in some degree probable....

and later on the same page:

I should think from the facts communicated to me by Mr. Blyth....whose opinion, from his large and varied store of knowledge, I should value more than that of almost anyone....

We might well ask: Who are these people, what are their credentials, where and when did they write or say these things?

Darwin does not have a note in his book (in my Hutchinson & Co., London, 1906 edition). Further, the mass of evidence in Darwin's *Origin* is evidence for the existence of evolution, not its cause, or origin.

Darwin did provide proper references for his other books, so perhaps we can deduce he omitted them from *Origin* because he was in a hurry to publish it to be sure Wallace was not somehow able to have this theory published first.

Whatever we may think of how Darwin and his influential friends behaved, Darwin published his *Origin of Species by Means of Natural Selection Or the Preservation of Favoured Races in the Struggle for Life* in November, 1859, about 18 months after he received the Wallace paper. Darwin had amassed an incredible amount of evidence, and Wallace had worked out the theory. The combination as put together by Darwin rocked the theological world and became a best seller with the public. Bishop Wilberforce and Thomas Huxley (another friend of Darwin) had a famous public debate on evolution. Since then, so called "Darwinism" or evolutionary theory has become the conventional wisdom.

CHAPTER 2

IS THIS EVOLUTION?

40 MILLION YEARS AGO?

One representation of the legacy of Darwinism comes from an excellent popular book put out by Reader's Digest. It's called The Last Two Million Years. I can thoroughly recommend it.

But I have some serious problems with this conventional approach to "evolution." First, the book itself: There are 488 pages in this book. But on page 28 what we find is a stone wall excavated at Jericho, dated to 8000 years ago. The text really begins on page 10, and on page 11 it says: "Since Darwin shocked the world with his theory that men and apes have a common ancestor, experts have pieced together the likely pattern...."

So the book has:

18 pages on the first 1,990,000 years = 0.5%

461 pages about the last 10,000 years = 99.5%

This shows how little we understand human life on earth more than 10,000 years ago.

The book gives us an opening illustration of the evolutionary theory as applied to humans.

Here are the first four of the eight "ancestors" of present day mankind according to this book,

From left to right these are listed as:

Common Ancestor
Ramapithecus
Australopithecus
1470 Man

What is said to be the 'Common Ancestor,' about 40 million years ago or before present (40 MYBP) is described this way:

a forest dwelling primate moving on all fours, the ancestor from which modern apes and man both descend. But no traces of such a creature have yet been found.

If that's the case, why is it here? So let's eliminate this purely hypothetical creature.

Next we are said to be at 14 million years ago, and we meet an artist's impression of Ramapithecus. Believe it or not, this type of reconstruction was based on the merest bits and pieces of old bone and two pieces of upper jaw bone. Here's what they look like:

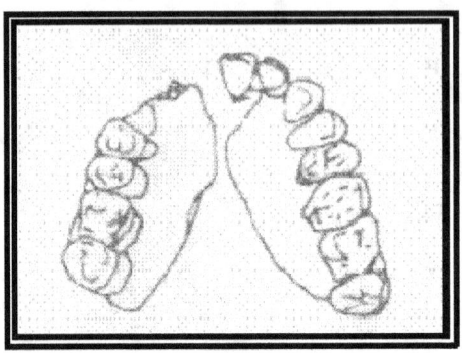

There's more to it than that. These fragments weren't found like that. They were put together in that way to resemble a modern human jaw bone which is like this:

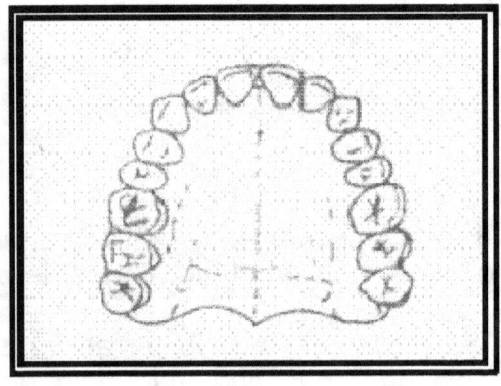

But since then, a whole Ramapithecus lower jaw bone has been found, and it looks like this:

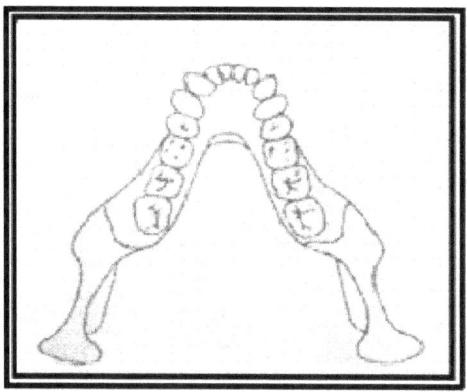

And here's a modern chimpanzee's lower jaw:

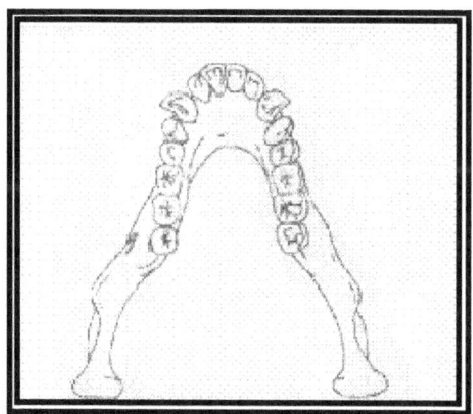

Although all three examples have sixteen teeth it seems fairly obvious that Ramapithecus was some kind of ape, from the only hard evidence we have. So let's drop Ramapithecus, and see what we have next.

Now we are down to 5 million years ago and we are looking at another "artist's impression", this time of Australopithecus. He's the third from the left in our first (four part) image. This is still conjectural. All we have left are pieces of bone. It "probably" used tools we're told. We have no evidence for that either, but if we are to have an evolutionary theory, it makes it flow better. The creature is described as a

man-like ape , whose brain was no larger than that of a modern ape.

What scholars have apparently done is take a number of different looking finds in different places over a period of from about 4 million years ago down to about 1 million years ago and lump them all together as 'Australopithecines'. The 'species' in this 'genus' are generally said to be:

Million years before present (MYBP):

Australopithecus	Afarensis	3.6-3
A "	Africanus	2.5-3
A "	Africanus/Habilis	2.5-3
A "	Boisei	1.8
A "	Robustus	1.5-2

They have all apparently been extinct a million years or more now.

Here's one of them: A Boisei (or zinjanthropus):

It has a high ridge or crest on top of the skull. That's what gorillas have today. The reason is said to be because they have massive jaws, used for chewing vast amounts of plant matter. The jaws are hooked by muscles on to the ridge.

So let's drop A Boisei as a gorilla type of ape (no man has a ridge like that), and look at A. Robustus:

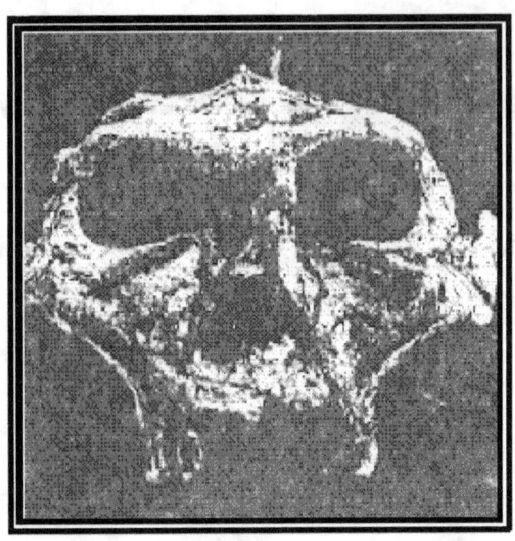

This is another specimen with a gorilla-type head ridge. So I suggest we discard it.

That eliminates the two younger extinct 'species'. Now we're left with

A. africanus 2.5-3 MYBP
A. africanus/habilis 2.5-3 MYBP
A. afarensis 3-3.6 MYBP

the older 'species'.

Africanus is calculated to have a cranial brain case capacity of about 425-480 ccs (cubic centimetres).

Afarensis had a cranial capacity of about 400 ccs, and stood about 4 ft. tall -- if it stood at all.

The skull formations of all the Australopithecenes (A) are very ape-like, and the cranial capacity is very small. The calculated range is 420 - 485 ccs.

If we compare that with living apes: chimpanzees, orangutans and gorillas, this is what we get:

Cranial capacities (cubic cm.) of living Hominoides (Ashton and Spence 1958, Martin and Saller 1959):

SAMPLE	HOW MANY	MEAN CCs
Pan Troglodytes (Chimps.)		
Male	33	410
Female	78	380
Pooled	111	390
Pongo Pygmaeus (Orang.)		
Male	30	415
Female	16	370
Pooled	48	400
Gorilla Gorilla		
Male	63	550
Female	50	460
Pooled	113	510
Homo Sapiens (Humans)		
Male		1317-1609
Female		1181-1445

For Homo Sapiens the 'Range of Means' is said to have been for 37 populations.

We can see at once that all these ancient extinct creatures fall in the range between the largest and smallest living apes. Mankind has a cranial capacity about three times the brain case capacity of any ape and is therefore quite different. It seems to me fair to deduce that these 2.5 - 3.6 million year old creatures were all apes of one kind or another. It's true they had some different qualities from living apes, but that may be merely a response to the different conditions of those far off times.

CHAPTER 3

WHOSE FOOTPRINTS?

In equatorial east Africa some footprints have been found --
they are about 3.5 million years old, calculated by the
potassium-argon dating method:

Whatever made the footprints on the left walked on two feet, and the feet have an arch, toes and a rounded heel. This small individual at the left is calculated to have been about 3'10" tall (1.2 metres). Because the larger track is said to have a smaller one stepping in it, heights cannot be calculated for those prints. Something with a human-like foot was walking through volcanic ash, upright and barefoot, 3.5 million years ago. Whether this was any of the Australopithecenes we just don't know.

At first you might think these were very like human footprints. But the smaller prints on the left are splayed out at an angle of about 42 degrees which probably means the creature was bent forward at the waist like an ape walking on two legs. We walk with our feet pointing almost straight ahead. And it's just possible that the larger prints are double because the creature on the right used its knuckles or hands as it walked on all fours. The smaller footprints to the left match the stride and placement of the larger ones to the right. This is something one would not expect of a child today walking beside an adult, unless deliberately doing so for fun. But this was probably not a fun situation. The makers of the footprints may have been trying to escape from the source of the volcanic ash. The ash on the ground may have been hot, and this is then the reason for not walking on all fours.

The smaller prints in the larger ones, if made by a separate creature, may have been because the heat was less once the larger foot had absorbed some of the heat and the larger creature may have provided some protection from searingly hot wind or rain.. The volcano is today identified as Sadiman, about 20 kilometres to the east of the footprints. Unfortunately we are not told the direction of the prints in relation to the volcano. We should be able to reconstruct the scene using our modern experiences with significant volcanic eruptions at Krakatoa, Mount St. Helens and Montserrat. One further point is that the smaller prints to the left are so close to the larger ones that they are less than the length of the larger foot away. This would seem to make walking together difficult if the prints were made at the same time, and if, as is said, the smaller creature was almost 4 feet tall.

The small tracks to the extreme right are said to be those of an extinct three-toed horse. Its tracks are not parallel to the footprints.

As the footprints and fossil remains of various animals we are told

are similar in type to the animals found in the area today....

....antelopes, hares, giraffes, rhinoceroses, horses, pigs and elephants

it's quite possible in my view that the hominid footprints were made by precursors of bonobos, a type of chimpanzee living in Africa today that frequently walks about upright and has been filmed carrying food bundles under one arm as it walks on two feet. But great apes are not human beings.

CHAPTER 4

LUCY WHO?

The famous partial skeletal remains of "Lucy" are dated to about 3 million years ago. We are told 'she' was about 3'7" tall, 25-30 years of age, and she walked upright. The pelvic bone structure is much narrower than in a human female and would presumably only allow the passage of a much smaller brain case for an infant:

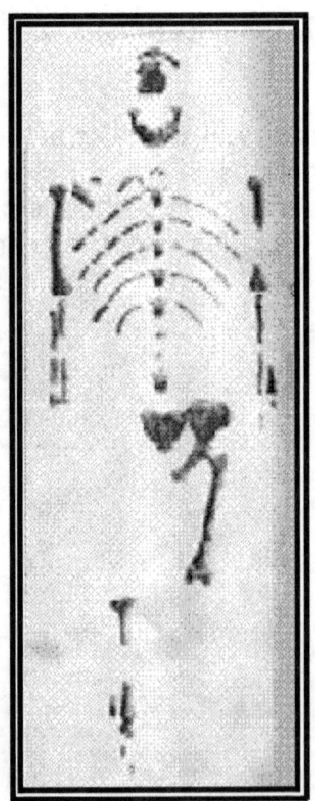

And this is the reconstruction:

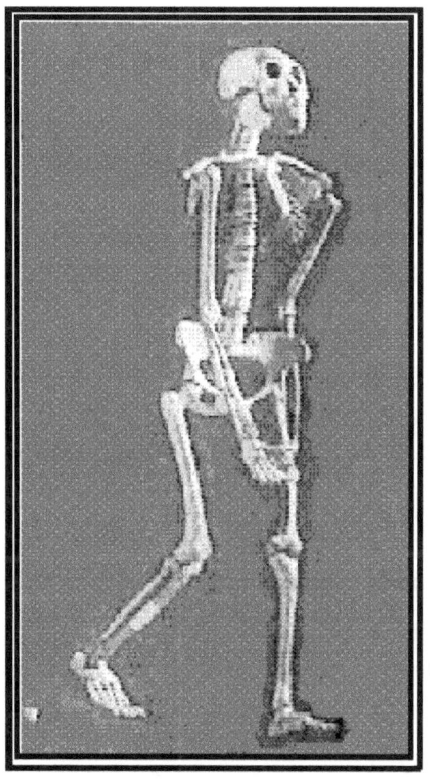

Lucy was found in an area in Africa over 1,000 miles (over 1,700 km.) northeast from where the footprints were found, and either could be plus or minus 150,000 years from the other.

"Lucy" was a remarkably complete skeleton for something that could be as old as 3.2 MYBP. The technical name is A Afarensis as she was found in the Afar region of Ethiopia. The arms are unusually long and she had curled fingers, so the creature was probably adept at tree climbing, as well as able to walk upright (although one anthropologist has argued she was only able to keep her balance if she walked with her hip joint flexed like a chimpanzee). The jaw is V-shaped like a chimp and some teeth have ape like features.

We should be very careful when all we have to work with is bones. One problem with "Lucy" was to tell which bits belonged to her and which didn't.

Here are two examples of difficulties when working with bones only:

Can you tell which is from a 3 - 3.5 MYBP "first family" of Australopithicenes and which from a 50 MYBP lemur? (a nocturnal monkey-like creature with a pointed muzzle):

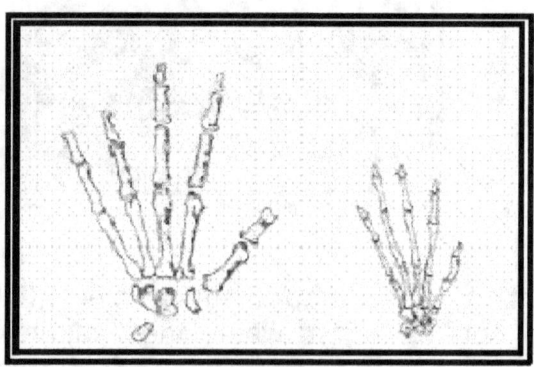

The lemur hand is on the right.

And here's a present day example: can you tell which are bear paws and which are human hands?

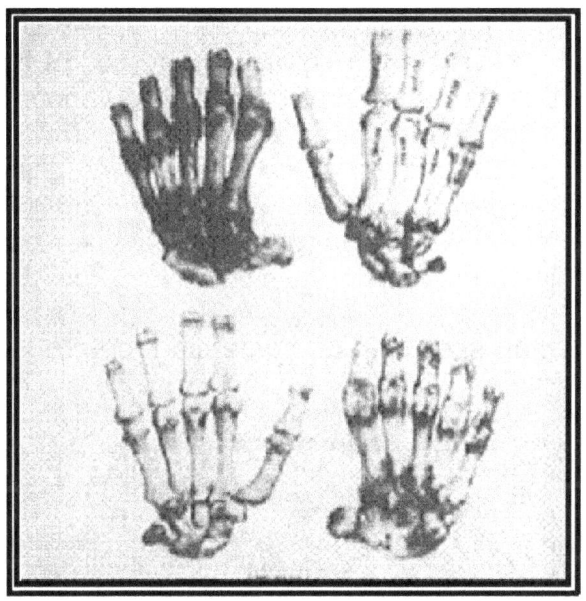

The bear paws are top left and lower right. Were you correct?

So let's leave the Australopithecenes as they all seem to have been apes of one kind or another. There was no advantage in walking upright with a brain case the size of that of a chimpanzee or a gorilla because any similar sized 4-footed creature could probably run you down in no time -- even chimps and monkeys can sprint faster than humans today.

CHAPTER 5

Mr. 1470

Let's see who is next on our illustration of evolution (chapter 2): something from about 2.5 MYBP. You can see that straight line evolution is not working here because '1470 man' is as old as some of the Australopithecenes. All that exists is the skull of 1470 -- so called because it is catalogued as #1470 in the Kenya National Museum in Nairobi. It was "painstakingly reconstructed (by an anatomist) from hundreds of fragments". There are problems with its date. These are variously 2.9, 1.8 and 1.6 MYBP. It seems probable the 1.8 - 1.6 MYBP dates are correct. It was found at Koobi Fora. The 1470 find at Koobi Fora was about halfway between the Olduvai Gorge area and the Afar site, where Lucy was found in Ethiopia. Koobi Fora is about 500 miles from each.

I am somewhat skeptical of something put together from hundreds of fragments, but this is the result we are given:

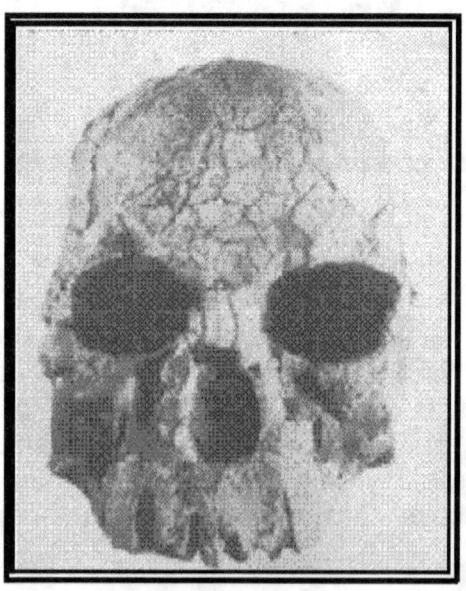

The cranial capacity of the 12 or so specimen remains of this type of 'near-man' are given as 600-850 ccs.(cubic centimetres) 1470 is given as 775 ccs.

Here are the ccs of three more "homo habilis" or Latin for "handyman". (It seems to carry more prestige to translate the names into Latin). All the ccs are estimates:

Olduvai Hominid 7: 657
Olduvai Hominid 13: 640
Olduvai Hominid 16: 620

From the evidence of the brain case there seems to be no factual justification for calling this creature a man of any kind, 'handy' or not. But it fits the theory of evolution to postulate this kind of early development. It's true the 1470 skull as reconstructed looks surprisingly like modern man from the front, but here is another view of it with a modern skull to the right:

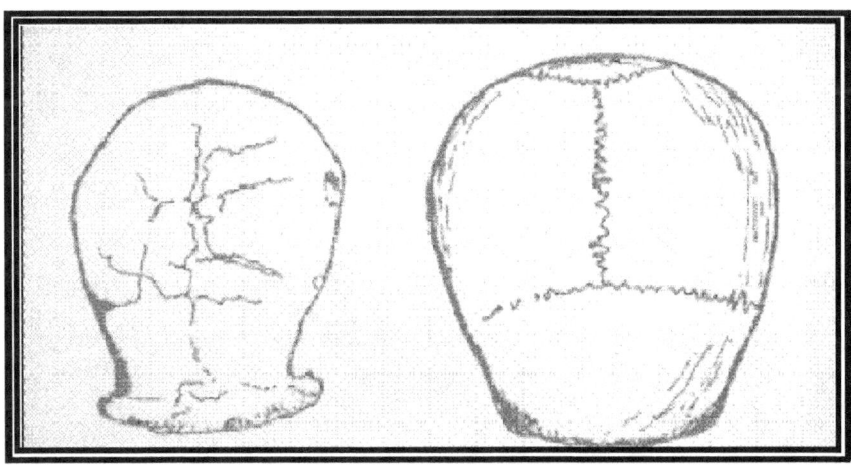

This view indicates that 1470 probably had massive jaw muscles and therefore massive jaws. And seen from the rear the skull seems to bulge out around the base, indicating heavy neck muscles necessary to hold a creature not fully erect. A human-looking thigh-bone found nearby may indicate erect posture, if it belongs to a 1470 type creature. Surprisingly (since teeth last longest) there are no teeth with 1470, and no other identifiable remains. This means that features as yet unknown at present could further solidify the case for 1470 being an early man-type, or could equally show him/her to be a possibly upright-walking ape.

My view is that this is the first serious candidate we have come across for a precursor of mankind today. But as it was put together from hundreds of parts by a modern man who must have forced the assembly in some way because the result is asymmetrical, and because all we have is part of a skull, and the top and back are not indicative of a modern skull, I think we should set it aside as an interesting development among ancestral apes that became extinct.

CHAPTER 6

FOUR HOMOS TO GO

It's time to have another look at the evolutionary illustration we started with. We have now more or less eliminated the first four items ranging from 40 million years ago to 2.5 (or 1.6) million years ago.

Let's see what's left - 4 more male specimens:

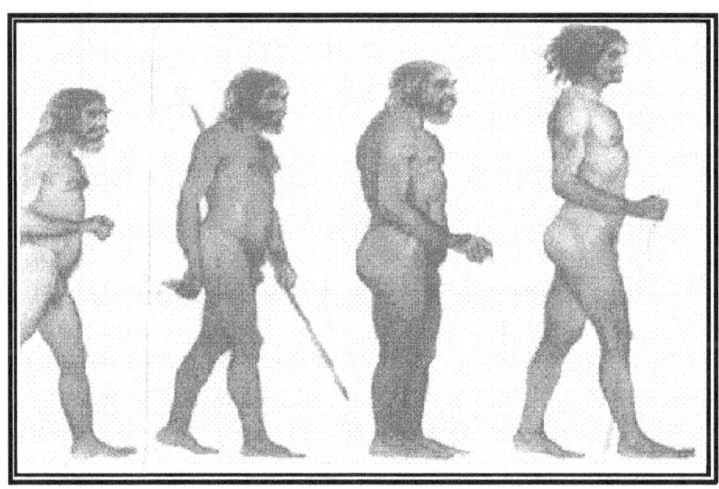

These are all 'artists' reconstructions', again from bones for all but the last specimen - unless he is meant to be from 35,000 years ago. They are captioned, from left to right (BP = before present):

Homo Erectus 500,000 BP

Homo Sapiens 250,000 BP

Neanderthal Man 70,000 BP

Modern Man from 35,000 BP

I suggest that they could be shuffled in any order. By that I mean if you look at height and face only, you might meet any one of them on a bus or subway train going to work, if suitably dressed, so the illustrations are presumably not accurate:

But this is not the point, and if that were all there was to it, we wouldn't be here looking at these very hypothetical reconstructions from all the bits of bone supposedly supporting the theory of evolution.

After all these millions of years we've been shown (but not properly on a time scale) the problem which our illustrated series of artist's impressions conveniently ignores:

how did we get from this only about 12,000 years ago:

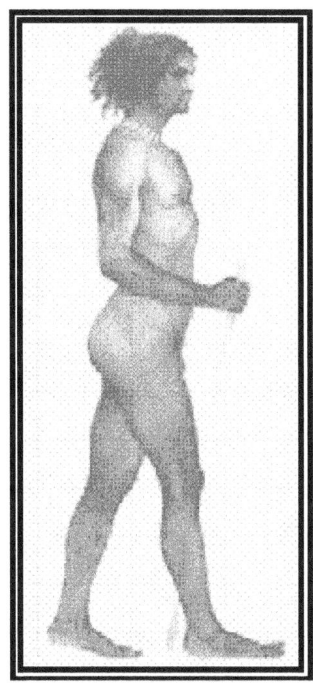

To this today? :

And that's a question the evolutionary theory seems to have no proper answer for.

We're not alone in having this problem. Alfred Wallace, described as 'even more rigorous than Darwin in applying the principle of natural selection' ... questioned its efficacy for humans.

If early hominids required only a gorilla's intelligence to survive, Wallace asked, why had they evolved brains capable of devising language, composing symphonies, and doing mathematics?

Although our bodies had evolved by natural selection, he concluded, Homo Sapiens has

"something which he has not derived from his animal progenitors - a spiritual essence or nature..."

CHAPTER 7

BRAINS

Let's come at this problem a different way. We're told that the DNA of chimpanzees is over 98% the same as ours. If so, then there's more to it than DNA because chimps don't compose symphonies or do mathematics; (Note 1). We don't have fur, only vestigial hair, except on our heads, we walk upright (bipedal) but our infants do crawl on all fours. Apes can walk upright but generally go on all fours. Apes are generally vegetarians, although chimps occasionally hunt and eat monkeys. Humans are generally carnivorous (meat eaters). Ape brain case capacity is about a quarter to a third of ours and their heads and limbs are shaped differently from ours.

When we try to trace our lineage back we can't tell whether hominids had fur or skin like ours, what they ate, even how they walked, but we can tell brain case capacity from fossils. It's true that female humans are slightly smaller in build than males. They have correspondingly smaller brain cases, but no one would argue that they have less brain power than males. Since females have entered professional accounting and competed with males in final exams in Canada, although far fewer in numbers than male candidates they have begun to equal males in the honours lists and as medallists. So a 10% smaller brain case does not necessarily mean 10% less brain power. Mentally retarded adults still have normal-sized brain cases. The organization of the internal structure of the brain and our inherent mental ability is then at least as important as overall size. But, having noted these facts it is still statistically true to say that human brain cases are 3 to 4 times larger than that of the great apes living today. Bearing in mind these limitations, we are entitled to consider brain case size as a significant factor in determining whether a fossil skull, by its shape and size, is likely to have been a human or near-human (if there is such a creature) or if you prefer the Latin for humans, homo sapiens sapiens. How far back then, can we trace fossil brain cases similar in capacity to our own?

During the last 100 years pieces of fossil skulls and various bones that look somewhat human have been dug up by archaeologists or excavated by accident in various parts of the world. Apparently almost none of them are directly similar to each other unless found in groups. Each discovery of potentially human-like fossil remains was usually named after the place of discovery. Eventually this got out of hand. Instead, the phrase, Homo Erectus, or upright man, was coined to cover these different discoveries. Not all archaeologists, particularly those in France, agreed with this. For one thing, it contained the presumption that these were 'man,' homo being the latin word for man. But are we all descended from these various scattered half-million or so years old "homo erectus" specimens with a brain capacity of about 1,000 ccs or less?

At Fontechevade in S.W. France, in a cave, among twenty vertical feet of debris, was found an incomplete skull cap----its cranial capacity has been estimated as about 1465 ccs. Small pieces of a second skull indicated brow ridges as small as in European women today, quite unlike the heavy Neanderthal and ape brow ridges. Age is estimated between 85,000 and 135,000 years.

The Swanscombe specimen found in a gravel pit in Kent, in England, is said to be about 250,000 years old. It has an estimated cranial capacity of 1325 - 1350 ccs., virtually the same as for a modern human.

The slope at the rear of the skull was not squat and bun-shaped like Homo Erectus and Neanderthal. Fossil bone found near the skull (but not positively identified with it) has been radio-carbon dated to more than 272,000 years before present (BP).

The Steinheim skull was found in a gravel pit near Stuttgart, Germany. It has an estimated cranial capacity of about 1150 ccs -- at the low end of our present cranial capacity. The dating may be similar to that of the Swanscombe specimen.

At Vertesszollos in Hungary in the mid-1960s was found a single occipital (back of the head) bone and stone "tools" associated with it. From this bone the cranial capacity has been estimated to be between 1405 and 1600 ccs. (Our present day average is about 1350 ccs.) This fossil is said to be between 400,000 and 700,000 years old.

I suggest we discount the accuracy of the Hungary specimen. When there is no skull cap to work with, the calculation of cranial capacity must be based on certain assumptions which may or may not be correct. Even without the Hungarian fossil we have a time sequence from say, about 100,000 years ago through 250,000 years ago with estimated cranial capacities entirely within our present human range.

What this presumably does is rule out the idea of the low-brain-size descendants of the batch of various primates grouped together as Homo Erectus having preceded modern man as potential ancestors. They are ruled out because the fossil record we have listed above precedes some of these other so-called ancestors. A more appropriate view might be that there is a sequence of high brain capacity individuals continuing at least several hundred thousand years into the past.

Instead of our own evolution from 'homo erectus' we seem to have certain ancient primates with a brain capacity up to about twice that of living apes, but who in half a million years did no more than use simple flint tools, hunt, and use fire. Apart from the use of fire, this places them not much above the level of existing chimpanzees who hunt in groups with considerable skill and use a variety of specially selected tools.

What we seem to find is a series of apes of different sorts and sizes between 5 million and 1.5 million years ago. As we have living great apes today, it appears logical to conclude that the long-ago apes were the precursors of our living apes. Then there is apparently a gap of over a million years after which from about 500,000 years ago down to about 35,000 years ago appear a few humanoid fossils with brain cases resembling present human size. But all they accomplished seems to have been creation of simple stone tools and possible use of fire.

This information may be helpful in understanding the ancestry of our living great apes, as part of the animal world, but none of it, I suggest, tells us how we came to be what we are. As human beings, we are quite different in abilities and achievements.

NOTE 1

On December 7, 2002 the National Post daily newspaper in Toronto page A2 carried a headline:

Humans share 99% of genes with mice

This came from a report by a group of scientists published in the scientific journal Nature. There, the Post stated, it was said that humans shared all but 300 of a total package of 30,000 genes with mice.

To this I would add that we are certainly very different from mice, so genes cannot be as important a differentiating factor as scientists apparently suggest. What we do have in common is that all three species, humans, mice and chimps, are mammals. All three have one heart, one blood supply, one nose, one mouth, one stomach, one liver, and one central nervous system; two ears, two eyes, two lungs, two legs and two arms or equivalent for mice. That is at about the level in which we are similar, so it would seem this is probably the level at which the genes are operating, and therefore has very little to do with anything beyond the cerebellum/hippocampus level of the brain. It seems to be the size and content of the advanced brain, the cerebrum, resting above the lower level which apparently makes us human at our present level.

It may be, then, that mammals all began with the same physical template and were endowed with or developed niche characteristics which make us and maintain us at levels of specialization that we now possess.

Mice may not be able to build or fly a plane at supersonic speed, but few if any humans could master 300 turns of a maze in three days to find a piece of cheese in the middle.

CHAPTER 8

2003

In the June 12 issue of Nature, an international weekly journal of science, an article and correspondence was published relating to a find in Africa of some fossils said to be the earliest homo sapiens. Because Nature is primarily for specialists, much of the language used is scarcely intelligible to non-specialists. More popular magazines such as Scientific American have their own writers who summarize and translate the articles of general interest into more familiar English.
Here's an example of the language in the article:

The supraorbital torus is differentiated into halves at the level of the (multiple) supraorbital foramina. The flat lateral portion is extremely broad anteroposteriorly (at zygofrontal suture 18 mm from orbital rim to temporal line), and forms a superoanteriorly facing trigone.

From another source here's an explanatory diagram which may help:

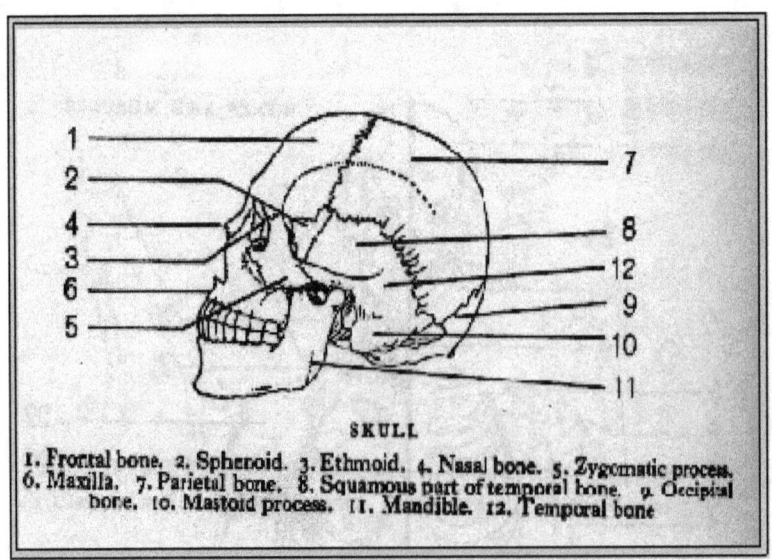

SKULL

1. Frontal bone. 2. Sphenoid. 3. Ethmoid. 4. Nasal bone. 5. Zygomatic process. 6. Maxilla. 7. Parietal bone. 8. Squamous part of temporal bone. 9. Occipital bone. 10. Mastoid process. 11. Mandible. 12. Temporal bone

However, there is sufficient plain language for us to understand what is going on, and on that and our own translation abilities, such as they are, we will rely. Quotations will be in italics. My notes and comments will be in regular type.

The article was published as a very long letter, with seven scholars' names attached, which may mean they obtained publication but not financial reward for their contribution.

WHAT WAS FOUND?
1. *The most complete specimen so far recovered ...is an adult cranium,... exposure before recovery led to the loss of the left side of the calvarium...*
calvaria is Latin for skull.

The entire right facial skeleton is present...
Skeleton = bony structure of the skull.

There is some limited distortion in the existing remainder of this skull. And now we come to the reason why this chapter is being written.

The cranium, interpreted here as male, is generally large and robust, with a cranial capacity estimated by teff seed volume [right side doubled] at about 1,450 cm³, at the high end of the modern human range.
The great length of the cranium ...(globella to occipital) (219.5 + or - 2 mm) exceeds that found in... a global sample of over 3,000 modern humans...
The large overall size of (#1) stands out ... Apart from its exceptionally great anterior - posterior length
they mean front to back

the cranium exhibits large vault dimensions together with a deep, tall and broad face ... indistinguishable from anatomically modern homo sapiens [AMHS]...

This was no ape. All the ancient ancestors found so far of modern apes had brain cases well under 500 cubic centimetres (CCs); some living chimps have just over 400 ccs and gorillas under 600 ccs.

2. The second major adult specimen was an even larger adult, as judged by matching parts of its preserved temporal bone...the cranium, also a probable male, was highly fragmented and scattered after it emerged from the same sand unit. The lack of recovered dental, facial or basicranial parts indicates that it may have been embedded as a calotte.

A 'calotte' is a skull cap.

Evidence of intensive bone modification is present on 15 of its 24 recovered fragments. Some exhibit cutmarks that are probably associated with removal of soft tissue. Deep, typical defleshing cutmarks are seen on the parietals (the parietals are the two bones forming part of the sides and top of the skull) *left zygomatic* (bony part of the cheek) *frontal and occipital* (back of the head), *More abundant but more superficial marks showing a repetitive scraping motion are present around the vault circumference, above the nuchal* (nape of the neck) *and temporal lines* (the tempora is the flat side of the head between the forehead and ear). *The latter pattern of bone surface modification is almost never present in hominid or non human faunal remains processed for consumption, and is therefore unlikely to represent evidence of utilitarian or economic behaviour.*

3. A third adult individual represented by a left parietal fragment ... might have been slightly smaller overall than the two adults.

4. The immature cranium was found on the surface after its erosion ... it had been shattered into more than 180 small fragments from which the cranial vault and facial portions were restored... on the basis of modern human standards, we estimate the individual's age at death as 6-7 years. ...As with the adults the Herto child exhibits a character complex that is distinctly unlike that of Neanderthals.

WHERE WERE THESE SKULLS FOUND?
Here we report on stratigraphically associated Late Middle Pleistocene artefacts and fossils from fluvial and lake margin sandstones of the Upper Herto Member of the Bouri Formation, Middle Awash, Afar Rift, Ethiopia.

HOW LONG AGO DID THEY LIVE?

On the basis of the combined stratigraphic, geochemical and radioisotopic evidence, the Upper Herto archaeological and paleontological remains are therefore securely constrained to be between 160 (+ or - 2) and 154 (+ or - 7) k yr old...
And from another scholar's commenting letter

The fossils are complete enough to show a suite of modern human characters, and are well constrained by argon-isotope dating to about 160,000 years ago.
WHAT DID THEY EAT?

Associated faunal remains indicate repeated, systematic butchery of hippotamus carcasses.

ANY EVIDENCE FOR HUMAN-LIKE SOCIETY?

Contemporary adult and juvenile homo sapiens fossil crania manifest bone modifications indicative of deliberate mortuary practices.

Adult #2 cranial fragments show selected defleshing cutmarks on the left ... and other more superficial artificial scoring above the left temporal line and across the occipital plane....

#3 child's cranium with defleshing cutmarks on the left spheroid, and right and left temporals and post-mortem polish on the parietals.

The juvenile cranium ... displays an unambiguous series of defleshing-related cutmarks on the basicranial surfaces of its splenoid

(compound bone between the temporal bone and the eye)
and temporal bones on both right and left sides. These fine but deep repetitive cutmarks were made by a very sharp, probably obsidian flake edge. Their locations, dimensions and directions ... indicate that this ... must have occurred after removal of the mandible. The intentional and deliberate removal of soft tissues such as basicranial vessels, nerves and muscles is therefore indicated.

The diverse bone modifications marking the three most intact Middle Awash Herto hominid crania indicate postmortem defleshing with stone tools in the Upper Pleistocene, in an archaeological context straddling the Acheulean and MSA...

The Pleistocene epoch lasted from around 1.8 million years to some 12,000 years ago. MSA = Middle Stone Age. We have more to say about Acheulean later in this chapter.

WHAT WAS THE LANDSCAPE LIKE?

A widespread erosional surface ...(was found)... with distinctive rounded pebbles and large bentonite clasts ...(with) small gastropod shells often present immediately above the ... pebble horizon (we interpret) as having been deposited marginal to a shallow freshwater lake.

I believe bentonite is a kind of clay, and clasts are broken pieces of older rocks. Gastropods are fresh or salt water molluscs, e.g. snails and limpets.

This erosional surface is immediately overlain by a volcanic clastic sandstone and gravel deposit that yielded all of the Herto hominid fossils...

WHAT KIND OF WILDLIFE?

The bulk of the vertebrate fauna also comes from this widespread sand unit and includes a derived extinct bovine, Kobus species, Thryonomys, Hippopotamus, Equus and Connochaetes. These taxa indicate the proximity of both aquatic and grassland habitat.

'Bovine' is an ox, so, an extinct ox; 'kobus species' are African antelopes and waterbucks; 'Thryonomys' is of the order of rodents, and thryonomys swinderianus is the great cane rat, grasscutter, common today in Africa south of the Sahara, usually 1-2 feet in body length plus 3-10 inch tail, males weighing close to ten pounds, so, large rats; 'equus' includes horse, ass and zebra; and 'connochaetes' are wildebeest and gnu.

WHAT KIND OF TOOLS WERE FOUND?

The ...Upper Herto archaeological assemblages vary spatially in their lithological and typological contents. The Levallois method is well represented across samples ... and was used frequently in the production of the hand axes and cleavers. Evidence of Levallois method is also observed on 48 flakes, blades, and points,,, flakes are mostly elliptical with flat section, with platforms almost always faceted convex... with a platform angle always between 90° and 95°...

The analysed 28 bifaces span a wide size range and were all made on fine-grained basalt. They are represented by ovates, elongate ovates, triangulars, cleavers, and a pick, biface scraper and biface nucleus. The 17 hand axes with ovate and elongate ovate plan forms were always made on flakes and finished with soft hammer technique. Edges are regular and show secondary edge retouching.

The Acheulean is a style of stone tool-making attributed to 'homo erectus' or upright man. This 'man' is derived from a number of independent finds of prehistoric apelike creatures of somewhat different sorts and sizes from various sites around the world lumped together under a general heading of homo erectus. The largest brain case size of any of them was 1,000 ccs, in contrast with the 1450 ccs of the Upper Herto finds we are discussing here. One source book I have gives this sample of Acheulean tools:

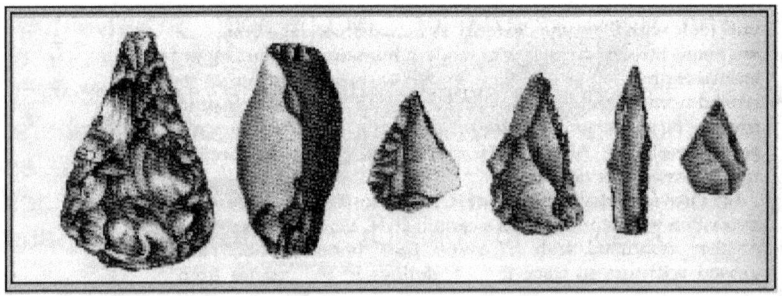

And describes them as:

Chipped hand axe, scrapers, blades and a point made by homo erectus between 1 million and 400,000 years ago, belonging to the Acheulian style

Another source book gives this sample

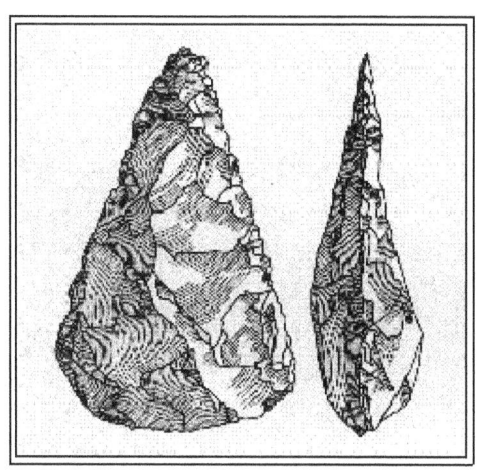

with the caption

Stone hand-axes, which were much more versatile than simple pebble-tools, were developed by 'Homo erectus' or 'Upright man,' who first appeared about half a million years ago. Their sharp points and edges were achieved by patiently chipping away a succession of thin flakes with a piece of bone or hard wood.

This is, I believe, the Levallois method described in the Nature article. A third source book provides these:

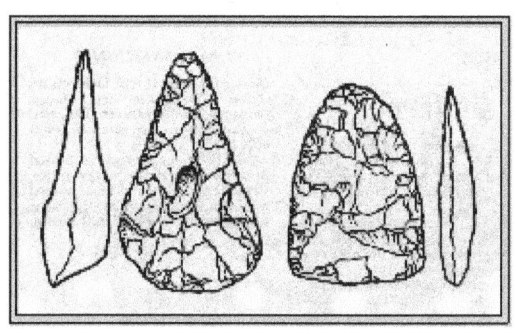

Described as (on the left)
Hand axe from Swanscombe, Kent, England, profile and front view, middle Acheulian

And (on the right) described as
Hand axe from Bournemouth, Hants. England, late Acheulian

You can see the late Acheulean has a slimmer profile, difficult to do with stone.

Once you get to flaking by use of softer material than stone there is little or no further significant development it seems to me even down to Neanderthal man as recently as 50,000 years before present:
I

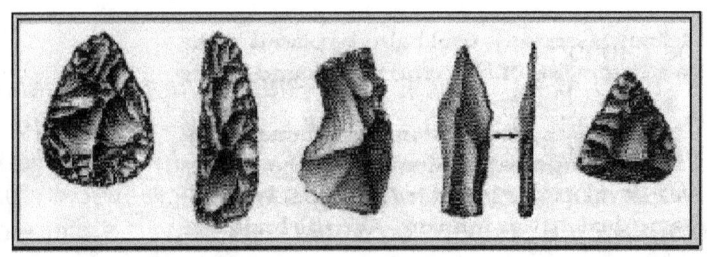

I have some problems with these illustrations. In the first two books cited the dates given for Homo Erectus are wildly different. Next, we have no provenance given for the tools illustrated, that is, we don't know where they came from, or whether they are individual pieces from different sources arbitrarily put together to present as a collection. We have no probable date for any of the finds and we don't know whether skulls were discovered with the finds, and if so, what were the ccs of their brain cases. As a consequence, I believe the illustrations provided may be interesting but not to be taken as reliable evidence for our purposes.Further, valuable as the Herto find is, although the 2nd letter/article says:

controlled surface collection and excavation at Upper Herto localities BOU-A19, BOU-A26 and BOU-A29 yielded a pooled lithic assemblage of 640 analysed artefacts (see Supplementary Information)...

I did not find the Supplementary Information identified as such in the article or by being appended to it. As a result, we do not have a photo of even one of these 640 stone tools so that we have no basis for comparison. I suggest scholars should provide better uniformity in presenting their work to the world.

WHAT DO SCHOLARS THINK OF THE HERTO FINDS?
Chris Stringer of the Human Origins Group, Natural History Museum, London, has this to say in a letter in the same issue of Nature:

Do the Herto fossils represent 'modern' H. Sapiens? ...despite the presence of some primitive features, there seems to be enough morphological evidence to regard the Herto material as the oldest definite record of what we currently think of as modern H. sapiens. The fact that the geological age of these fossils is close to some estimates obtained by genetic analyses for the origin of modern human variation only heightens their importance.

Tim D. White (Department of Integrative Biology and Laboratory for Human Evolutionary Studies, Museum of Vertebrate Zoology, University of California, Berkeley, California,) and his colleagues, who provided both letters to Nature, have this to say:

Because the Herto hominids are morphologically just beyond the range of variation seen in AMHS (Anatomically Modern Homo Sapiens) *and because they differ from all other known fossil hominids, we recognize them here as Homo Sapiens Idaltu , a new paleosubspecies of Homo Sapiens.*

GENERAL COMMENTS
In the description of the fauna, predators are not mentioned, and we have a very similar collection of vegetarian or herbivore animals to many of those living today in the grasslands of Africa near water sources.

Hippos (hippopotamus) are today a valued food source for many native Africans. The meat is highly prized, as is the fat, and the teeth yield superior ivory. The hide is also considered valuable.

Hippos live in large groups of 30 or more and spend the day time in water. At night they come ashore and graze on the grassland. They apparently all follow the same path to their feeding area and constant use can form almost a tunnel 5-6 feet deep. That's because hippos are so heavy. Adult males can weigh well over 4 tons. Their canine teeth can be up to 28 inches long, and their mouths can open 4 feet wide. The males fight for supremacy over females, sometimes to the death, and their hides have many scars from such conflicts. Defeated males may become solitary.

Confronting them 154-160,000 years ago in Ethiopia were human men with bigger brain cases than almost all the human population today. These people were expert hunters and experts with stone tools. They had a large tool kit and inventory which has survived until now. Their methods of production were not primitive. They had hand axes which require precision in chipping the basalt they used. Basalt is a fine grain igneous (volcanic) rock which can rise to the surface in fissures and faults. Basalt has about 40% silica, a glassy substance, so the tools would be sharp. They also used obsidian tools. Obsidian, another volcanic rock, has about 65% silica. When flaked it can be so sharp that a man can shave with it, or it can be used as a scalpel in surgery.

What particularly intrigues me is that these people had what the scientists call a pick. Here's a definition of a modern pick:

Tool consisting of an iron bar, usually curved with point at one end and point or chisel edge at other, with wooden handle passing through the middle perpendicularly, used for breaking up hard ground, masonry, etc. and in quarries etc.

We substitute basalt for iron bar and then we have a pick. What did they use it for? Depending on size it could have been used to remove nodules from rock formation for cores to be chipped into tools and flakes. Or it could have been used to break ground to dig a pit in the walkway of the hippos. I say that because how do men with stone hand tools kill a 4 ton hippo? One way would be to trap a single hippo in a concealed pit. As a hippo has small legs it would be at their mercy if in a pit from which it could not escape.

The 28 inch hippo ivory tooth could be hafted on to a pole to create a formidable pike or spear, something capable of killing a hippo. All that survives of their way of life is a very varied stone tool collection with some partial skulls and butchered hippo remains. We don't know what they did with the ivory or hide or available wood.

There are at least two peoples living today we might consider for comparison. First, the Bushmen of southern Africa, living in near-desert conditions. They are totally independent from civilization, and are skilful hunter-gatherers. Next, the Chukci nomads living well over 100 miles inside the arctic circle in north east Russia. It is very cold there. More extreme conditions can hardly be imagined on this planet. It's a frozen desert, These people live in small groups and each group is completely dependent on over 1000 reindeer. There is no vegetation, nothing green to see or eat. The reindeer dig down to find lichen. The Chukci eat and drink continuously and keep active. They use every part of the reindeer for sustenance. Their living quarters are a tent within a tent, with wooden poles (which at some time past must have been obtained further south) and covered with reindeer skins. When our civilization is no more, as has happened to all previous civilizations on every continent, these two peoples, the Bushmen and the Chuckci, can continue their way of life, uninterrupted and unaffected. They are not apes, they are intelligent human beings, with language, customs, traditions and expertise all their own.

One other factor may be mentioned. In the 20th century it is said that there were found tribes living in New Guinea described as stone age people. That is, they used stone tools exclusively. But they too are intelligent human beings with their own social customs, traditions and way of life.

I suggest that homo sapiens at Herto in Ethiopia about 155-160,000 years ago were very similar in their complete self-sufficiency, certainly in much more favourable conditions than the present day peoples I've described. I assume the Herto people used wood, bone and ivory as well as stone tools, had their own language, social customs and traditions. They too were intelligent human beings. Their major difference from us is that we are products of a series of relatively recent civilizations such that we can no longer survive in the wild in completely natural conditions. But today there are living intelligent human beings whose existence parallels that of the Herto people of long ago.

THE NEOLITHIC TRANSITION

There is another recent academic publication we should mention. This was published in late 2002. It included a book review by Dr. Stuart C. Brown, Professor of Archaeology in the Department of Anthropology, Memorial University, Newfoundland. Here's part of what he wrote:

...The problem is not how to explain the neolithic in West Asia but to explain it as a global phenomenon. After close to 5 million years of human physical and cultural evolution, neolithic transitions occur in Asia, Europe, Africa, and the Americas within a few thousand years of each other, a mere eyeblink in time. Are we to assume that there has been a global mental restructuring? I think not. The "prime movers"

which drove the neolithic in such disparate areas ...must be global in nature and right now a combination of environmental change and population growth seem to remain the most reasonable explanation.

This appears to be a very fair representation of contemporary scholarly opinion as to how humans changed from hunter-gatherers to agriculturalists in a relatively short space of time on various continents.

I suggest this view is mistaken. Because most scholars are imprinted with the Judeo-Christian belief and Darwinism, consciously or unconsciously, they look for evolving human abilities. In fact, as far as we can tell from the archaeological record there was little or no evolution in close to 5 million years except for some slightly more carefully chipped stone tools. That's why they have a problem with what used to be called the neolithic 'revolution.' In keeping with Darwinism this is now referred to as the neolithic 'transition.' But that doesn't change what actually happened. What ancient writers tell us is dismissed as myth or legend by our scholars. But I believe the ancient writers are telling us exactly what really happened, and it's time we listened to their words. Part of what they said is discussed in the next few chapters. Much more is quoted and discussed in the next episode in this series: The Immortals.

CHAPTER 9
THE GAP

What we will try to do here is narrow the gap, trace ourselves back from the present as far as we can to see if we can get a better grasp on what happened.

Going back two thousand years is no problem and shows that people then were much the same as we are today. Here's an actual man's head, complete with cap, recovered from a peat bog in Denmark which preserved it:

He is apparently clean shaven and looks the same as people today. We can go back much further than this. Here is a miniature ivory carving found in France, now dated to more than about 20,000 years ago:

There is nothing in the face of this carving to indicate anything basically different from the heads of people today.

We have cave art from the Dordogne area in south west France, east of Bordeaux, and the Altamira cave in north Spain c14 dated to about 14,800 BP. Many paintings are in vivid colours on cave walls or roofs, but here's a black and white copy of one at Fonte de Gaume in the Dordogne region. It's said to represent a male and female reindeer (remember the dates indicate it was during the last ice age):

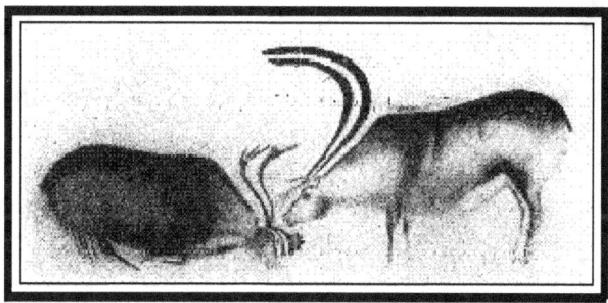

It seems probable that the Cro Magnon, or Late Neolithic people, whatever we want to call them, were the ones who carved the miniature ivory head we just saw, and created this cave painting. If so, they not only looked like us, they had equal or better artistic talent. We have one other carving, said to be about 26,000 years old. It comes from Czechoslovakia:

It's said to be male. If so, then he would appear to be clean shaven. The face is a noble face, and could belong to a person living today. This carving also shows us that 26,000 years ago there were artists who could produce works in no way inferior to that of our artists today, and, that human beings (who apparently did not have civilizations then) had the same skull structure as we do. They were "Cro Magnon" or "Homo Sapiens Sapiens" or "Modern" people. Cro Magnon skeletons have been found and they show taller people with larger brain cases than many people since down to the present day. Cro Magnon is a cave in the Dordogne area, and the words translate literally as 'big hole:'

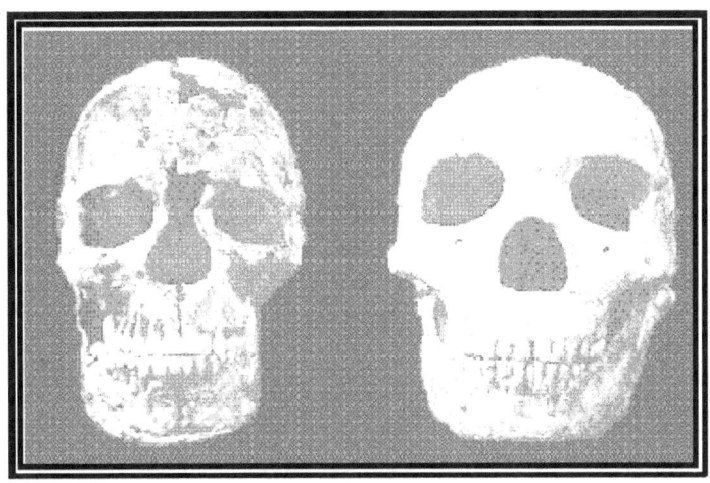

The modern human skull is on the left, with its high domed vertical forehead. That gives room for the frontal lobes which apparently are the areas of our highest co-ordinated intelligence. The skull on the right is Neanderthal. The Neanderthal skull is flatter and heavier and has more pronounced brow ridges projecting and stronger looking teeth.

A present-day dating technique shows the "modern" skull to be probably about 92,000 years old. The Neanderthal skull is much more recent, said to be probably more than 20,000 years younger, yet it is the Neanderthals that died out, perhaps in much the same way as mountain gorillas are said to be dying out in Africa today.

Neanderthal skulls have been found between about 36,000 years ago to close to 75,000 years ago. Tests on remains in Israel move 'modern man' back to 100,000 years BP and Neanderthal remains found in the same area to 120,000 BP. The skeletal remains and chipped stones associated with Neanderthals are said not to have changed appreciably during this time span. In fact the more recent remains are said to be among the most characteristically Neanderthal. This suggests cross-breeding with Modern Man was at the most minimal, now that we know Modern man can be traced back almost as far into the past as the Neanderthals.

A research paper on the speech of Neanderthals based on a computer assisted study of skulls shows that the constraints of the Neanderthal superlaryngeal vocal tract would make it impossible for him/her to produce "articulate" human speech....(They) could not produce vowels like a, i, u, or consonants like g or k. The conclusion of these and other researchers is that the Neanderthals were an early offshoot from the "hominids" before modern man. They are not apparently now considered in the direct line of descent to modern man.

An article by Christopher B. Stringer, (head of the Human Origins Group of the National History Museum in London, England) in Scientific American, December 1990 issue, provides two models of human past. Both begin at 700,000 BP and show Homo Erectus as universal around the world except that North and South America are omitted entirely.

Dr. Stringer then develops both models from 700,000 BP to the present. In both models each continent has its own precursors of a regional modern human: African, European, East Asian, and Australasian. Both models are identical to about 100,000 BP when his first model (the multi-regional) has the Neanderthals as ancestors of modern Europeans and Java as ancestral to modern Australasians. But at 100,000 BP his second model (the monogenesis) diverges by showing the Neanderthals, and the Java line (with a question mark), dying out while the African line expands to dominate and suffuse all the other three continents. Dr. Stringer presents arguments in favour of his second model and continues:

I believe that these observations support the monogenesis hypothesis: modern demographic patterns most probably began with the dispersal of early modern humans from Africa within the past 100,000 years.

Both lines of descent models showed 'Java' arising from Homo Erectus after 700,000 BP, later to perhaps become pre-Australasians within the last 100,000 BP. 'Java' is a 100 year old discovery by a Dutch doctor named Dubois. For many years there was great controversy over his find. He later concluded he had found remains of a giant extinct gibbon.

Of course, like everyone else in the field, Dr. Stringer is an evolutionist and so both his models begin with Homo Erectus. Later in the same article he says:

Modern humans and Neanderthals therefore seem to be distinct lines not diverged from a common ancestor more than 200,000 years ago----. The Moderns' alternate progenitors cannot yet be discerned in the fossil record.

So it seems to me the only reason we are tied in with Homo Erectus from 500,000+ years ago is that evolutionary theory requires us to have developed from something else. The bare facts seem to be that a progenitor has not been found for 'moderns' and there is no explanation of the cultural sophistication of modern humans in the past 30,000 years.

CHAPTER 10

ICE AGE OR GLOBAL WARMING?

The 'reindeer' cave art we saw in chapter 8 was located in southern France and there are certainly no reindeer there now. Reindeer are caribou, a sub-arctic animal. So as the big-brained human-like fossils go back some 300,000 years perhaps we should look at what our scientists tell us about the last ice age and its ending.

No one seems to know why it ended when it did; in fact there are various theories about how and why ice ages come and go. It has been recognized that oxygen isotope ratios vary with the volume of glacial ice. The earth also has magnetic field reversals from time to time, which can be identified. By taking deep sea cores and checking the oxygen isotope fluctuations against the magnetic polarity reversals, we get this:

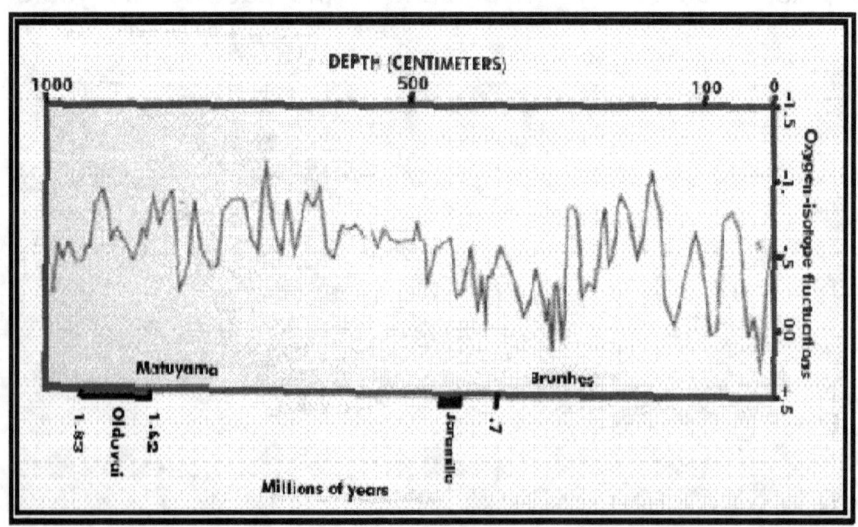

I prefer to read the scale horizontally as shown here, although it was originally vertical. Our present time is now at the right. Warm is up, cold is down. The horizontal time span is almost 2 million years. You can see that we are now reaching a peak of temperature after a climb from the last ice age. That climb is longer than any other in the last 1.9 million years, which suggests we are in for falling temperatures towards another ice age fairly soon. Temperatures have on average been in decline over the last 300,000 years. We can also note that the swings between warm and cold spells are becoming much more severe than they were earlier in the last two million years or so. Present conventional wisdom tells us the last ice age ended about 10,000 BP or at most started its decline about 12,000 years ago. If so, this chart may be of limited value unless the 10-12,000 BP change was too small or too recent to register, because by actual measurement it appears to me from the time scale given that the low point occurred at just over 30,000 BP and temperature has been rising since then.

As the interglacial ages advance, the amount of water in the oceans and elsewhere becomes correspondingly greater, producing a terraced effect, like this:

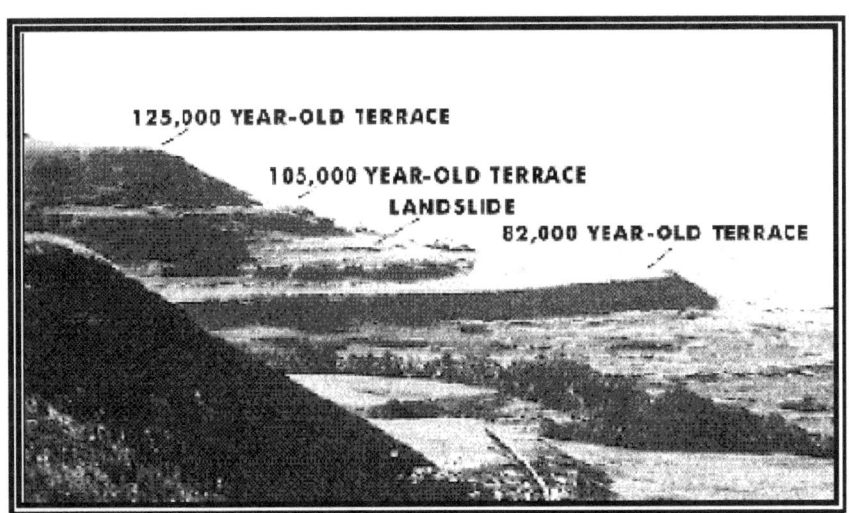

When the ice increases the sea levels go back down.

What this means is that as the planet is at present in a warm spell with sea levels rising, much low lying land is flooded that was inhabited during or soon after the end of the last ice age. Even Roman docks and wharves in the Mediterranean can be seen under water today. Land also rises when the weight of ice melts off it, and continents are always drifting about. So our planet has plenty of change and surface movement.

When we consider the time scale of ice ages against the known specimens of big-brained individuals, say back to about 300,000 years ago, we see they can be traced to the peak of a warm period and their history since then has spanned three ice ages and three warm periods. But during all that time it is apparently only in the last 5,000 to 6,000 or so years that urban civilizations have arisen.

CHAPTER 11

CHANGING THE CEREALS

There were two stages in the creation of civilizations. First came the domestication of plants and animals. This occurred shortly after the end of the last ice age. Radio carbon datings show that maize, or corn, was being cultivated in the Olmec-Maya area about 8,000 to 9,000 years ago.

There is, apparently, much argument but no proof yet as to what wild plant was used from which to develop corn. Corn was altered so that it could no longer propagate itself without the intervention of humans.

We know that wheat and barley, for example, were domesticated in the Near East around the foothills area of what is Iraq today, by about 6,750 BCE (Before Christian or Common Era), say 8,750 BP. In the case of wheat this was no simple transformation. The chromosomes were first doubled from 14 to 28 and then increased to 42. This wheat is still used for bread wheat today. The 'rachis' or stem was altered so that wheat could no longer propagate by itself. It needs planting by humans now, to grow, as the grains can no longer disperse over a distance.

According to one famous prehistorian the prehistory of rice cultivation is very obscure. He thinks it probably began earlier in India than in China. He also tells us that the origin of the humped bull (a universally domesticated ox to this day in India) is obscure, no wild species is known.

With such evidence as we have for crop and animal domestications, it seems reasonable to say that at about 8,000 to 9,000 years ago domesticated cereals, fruits and vegetables, and domesticated animals (goats, sheep and oxen) were being produced in Central America, the Near East and the Far East, in at least some cases involving changes in genetic structure, nearly all of which have remained unchanged since then. These changes were made to wild things shortly after the end of the last ice age and in widely separated parts of the world.

CHAPTER 12

WHERE DID CIVILIZATION COME FROM?

About two thousand years ago probably 100,000 people in what we now call Mexico were living in a magnificent city with many ziggurats or stepped pyramids, or temples. The city was called Teotihuacan, ("City of the Gods"). Here's one artist's impression as to what part of it looked like. It was in colour, not black and white as shown here:

Close to 4,000 years ago other people were living in cities in the Near East whose names are famous to this day: Babylon, Ebla, Eridu, Luxor, Thebes, Ur and Uruk. Here's an artist's impression as to how part of Babylon looked, although it was in vivid colours:

There were other ancient cities, for example in the Indus Valley area of what we now call the sub-continent of India: such as Mohenjo Daro and Harappa over 4,000 years ago.

In many of those cities, bricks were baked before laying, just as we use baked bricks today. That's why some of their brickwork still stands today. The houses of the Indus valley cities and Minoan cities were connected to main drainage, something many much later cities, such as in the European Middle Ages over 3,000 years later were lacking. It is evident that these very early cities had very carefully planned systems and architectural and engineering know-how.

The merchants of Mohenjo-Daro used seals to identify their property being shipped, to seal it for protection against theft and to certify documents. They were distinctive and sophisticated seals.

Seals were also used in the Near East, and in Central American cities. If we go back another 6,000 or 7,000 years beyond that, to, say 10,000 to 11,000 years ago, we have found no evidence for urban civilizations and the few people on earth in those days are thought to have lived in huts or caves.

What caused this remarkable advance into civilization in so short a time? Evolutionary theory can't explain it. We've already seen how the evolutionary theory is presented in a series of artist's impressions. Instead of an evolutionary path to man from forty million years ago to the present, I suggest we have only the last 300,000 years to consider. Even this is a very long period of time when we realize civilizations seem to have begun only about 5,000 to 6,000 years ago.

This "evolutionary path" in theory doesn't explain how there was hardly any progress for over 300,000 years, and then in the last few thousand years, we got from this, the most advanced technology of say, 30,000 years ago (with a one cent piece for size comparison):

to this, the US nuclear weapon command:

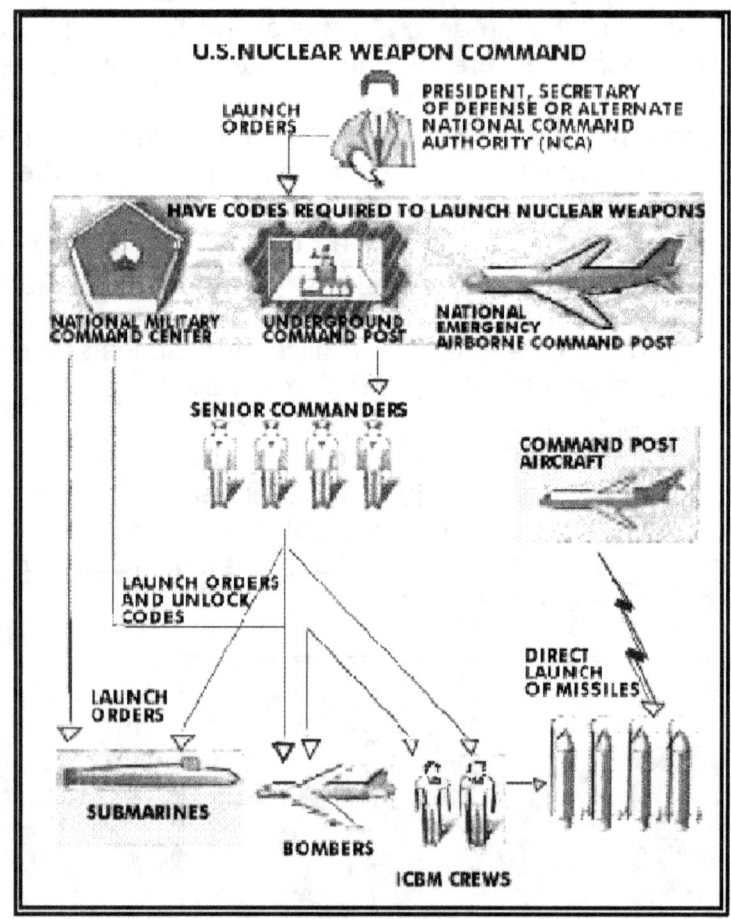

CHAPTER 13

KING LISTS AND GOD LISTS

The ancient Egyptians had a Pharonic King List, now called the Turin Canon, written on the reverse side of a tax list. It is possibly dated in the 1200s BCE. It has nothing to do with Turin except that it now resides in that city in Italy, and the word 'canon' generally refers to a papal decree or ecclesiastical law, so the name is somewhat misleading. Apparently it survived over 3,000 years intact, but was shipped unwrapped in a box to Italy by 'archaeologists' and arrived in a thousand pieces. As a result, much of it is missing but here are a few pieces that can be read:

First Column
Geb his life time(?) time of his reign being 733 (years)
Osiris (gap)
Seth (lost)
Horus of the Gods 300 years
Thoth 7,726
Maat 200
Horus (?)
A total of kings - (gap)

All these (except the last Horus - a semi- or half god) are gods.

Second Column

(?)	*1,110*		*years*
(?)			
?	*(a*	*thousand*	*something)*
(?)			

(?)

The glorified spirits the followers of Horus 13,420

(?) ...down to the followers of Horus 23,200 +

After this comes a King List of Egyptian Pharaohs recognized by scholars. The total of this "God List" such as it is, with much missing, is 58,089 years.

Herodotus was a Greek historian who travelled to Egypt and talked with priests there in about 455 BCE. (Heracles is the Greek God the Romans called Hercules.) Here's part of what Herodotus said:

"Heracles is a very ancient god of the Egyptians. As they themselves say, it was 17,000 years to the time when Amosis began to reign since the twelve gods, whereof they hold Heracles to be one, were born from the eight.... The Egyptians and their priests showed that there had been 341 generations of men from the first king unto this last. Now three generations of men are an hundred years, thus in 11,340 years, they said that no god in the form of a man had been king."

Manetho was apparently an Egyptian priest in the 200s BCE. His three-volume work is lost but parts of it have come down to us as he is quoted by others.

Here's what we get from Manetho:

As Edited in the Third Century B.C.
by the
Egyptian Priest Manetho.

DYN. I OF GODS.	YEARS	YEARS
1. HEPHAISTOS — — — — — — — — —	9000	
2. HELIOS — — — — — — — — —	992	
3. AGATHODAIMON - — — — — — — —	700	
4. KRONOS - — — — — — — — —	501	
5. OSIRIS & ISIS — — — — — — —	433	
6. TYPHON (SET) — — — — — — —	359	11985
DYN. II OF GODS.		
7. HORUS — — — — — — — — —	100	
8. ARIES — — — — — — — — —	92	
I ANUBIS — — — — — — — —	68	
II HERAKLES — — — — — — —	60	
III APOLLO - — — — — — — —	100	
IV AMMON - — — — — — — —	120	
V TITHOES - — — — — — —	108	
VI SOSOS — — — — — — —	128	
VII ZEUS — — — — — — —	80	
Years wanting — — — —	2	858
		12843
DYN. III OF GODS.		
VIII { BYTES }	1056	1056
		13899
IX DYN. I. DEMI-GODS — — — — —	1255	
X DYN. II. " " — — — — —	1817	
XI DYN. III. " " (MEMPHIS) — —	1702	
XII DYN. IV " " (THIS) — — —	350	5124
		19023
MANES (GHOSTS) — — — — — —	5813	5813
17 SOTHIC CYCLES = 24,837		24836

With the exception of Osiris and Isis, Horus, Anubis, Ammon and Sosos, the names given for all the gods are Greek. The order of this appearance seems very confused when considered in relation to the Greeks own ideas of the lives of descent of their gods and goddesses.

We have no time-line for the Greek Immortals but the lines of descent are: from Gaea and Uranus these six brothers and their six sisters:

MALE	FEMALE
Oceanus	Theia
Coeus	Rhea
Hyperion	Themis
Iapetus	Mnemosyne
Kronos	Phoebe
Crius	Tethys

The above twelve Titans mated among themselves and had offspring, among them:

Kronos, who had a son named Zeus.

Zeus, some sons of his were :

Aries..Hyphaestos..Heracles..Apollo

And
Hyperion, had a son named Helios

We can see the order of kingship according to the Egyptians bears little relationship to the order of birth according to ancient Greek tradition. Each of these civilizations recognized and built temples to some of the gods recognized by the other.

Let's look at another civilization in the Near East -- the Sumerian-Babylonian, apparently the oldest of the Asian civilizations. Here we have another "king list":

When kingship was lowered from heaven, kingship
was (first) in Eridu. (In) Eridu, A-lulim[4] (became)
king and ruled 28,800 years. Alalgar ruled 36,000 years.
Two kings (thus) ruled it for 64,800 years.

I drop (the topic) Eridu (because) its kingship was
brought to Bad-tibira. (In) Bad-tibira, En-men-lu-Anna
ruled 43,200 years; En-men-gal-Anna ruled 28,800 years;
the god Dumu-zi, a shepherd, ruled 36,000 years. Three
kings (thus) ruled it for 108,000 years.

I drop (the topic) Bad-tibira (because) its kingship
was brought to Larak. (In) Larak, En-sipa-zi-Anna
ruled 28,800 years. One king (thus) ruled it for 28,800
years.

I drop (the topic) Larak (because) its kingship was
brought to Sippar. (In) Sippar, En-men-dur-Anna became king and ruled 21,000 years. One king (thus) ruled
it for 21,000 years.

I drop (the topic) Sippar (because) its kingship was
brought to Shuruppak. (In) Shuruppak, Ubar-Tutu became king and ruled 18,600 years. One king (thus)
ruled it for 18,600 years.

These are five cities, eight kings ruled them for 241,000
years. (Then) the Flood swept over (the earth).

After the Flood had swept over (the earth) (and)
when kingship was lowered (again) from heaven, kingship was (first) in Kish. In Kish, Ga[. . .]ur became
king and ruled 1,200 years—(original) destroyed! legi-
ble (only) to heavenly Nidaba (the goddess of writing)
—ruled 960 years. [Pala-kinatim ruled 900 years; Nan-
gish-lishma ruled . . . years];[5] Bah[i]na ruled . . . years;
BU.AN. [. .] . [um] ruled [8]40 ye[ars]; Kalibum ruled
960 years; Qalumum ruled 840 years; Zuqaqip ruled .
900 years; Atab ruled 600 years; [Mashda, son][6] of Atab
ruled 840 years; Arwi'um, son of Mashda, ruled 720
years; Etana, a shepherd, he who ascended to heaven
(and) who consolidated all countries, became king and
ruled 1,560 (var.: 1,500) years; Balih, son of Etana,
ruled 400 (var.: 410) years; En-me-nunna ruled 660
years; Melam-Kishi, son of En-me-nunna ruled 900
years; Bar-sal-nunna, son of En-me-nunna, ruled 1,200
years; Samug, son of Bar-sal-nunna, ruled 140 years;
Tizkar, son of Samug, ruled 305 years; Ilku' ruled 900
years; Ilta-sadum ruled 1,200 years; En-men-barage-si,
he who carried away as spoil the "weapon" of Elam,
became king and ruled 900 years; Aka, son of En-men-
barage-si, ruled 629 years. Twenty-three kings (thus)
ruled it for 24,510 years, 3 months, and 3½ days.

After the so-called "mythical" figures, the list goes on:

Kish was defeated in battle (lit.: was smitten with weapons), its kingship was removed to Eanna (sacred precinct of Uruk).

In Eanna, Mes-kiag-gasher, the son of the (sun) god Utu, became high priest as well as king, and ruled 324 years. Mes-kiag-gasher went (daily) into the (Western) Sea and came forth (again) toward the (Sunrise) Mountains; En-me-kar, son of Mes-kiag-gasher, he who built Uruk, became king and ruled 420 years; the god Lugalbanda, a shepherd, ruled 1,200 years; the god Dumu-zi, a šu.peš-fisherman'—his (native) city was Ku'a(ra),—ruled 100 years; the divine Gilgamesh, his father was a *lilla*,' a high priest of Kullab, ruled 126 years; Ur-Nungal (var.: Ur-lugal), son of Gilgamesh, ruled 30 years; Utul-kalamma, son of Ur-nun-gal (var.: Ur-lugal), ruled 15 years; Laba[h . . .]ir ruled 9 years; En-nun-dara-Anna ruled 8 years; MES(?).ḪÉ, a smith, ruled 36 years; Melam-Anna ruled 6 years; Lugal-ki-tun(?) ruled 36 years. Twelve kings (thus) ruled it for 2,310 √ years.

Uruk was defeated in battle, its kingship was removed to Ur.

In Ur, Mes-Anne-pada became king, ruled 80⁰ years; Mes-kiag-Nanna¹⁰ became king, ruled 36 years; [Elulu ruled 25 years; Balulu ruled 36 years. Four kings (thus) ruled it for 177 years. Ur was defeated in battle].

Then we have reached the age of Sargon, a known historical king. We can also see how the very long pre-flood reigns shrank to less than 10% after the flood and these gradually contracted down to normal spans for a reign in historical times. This phenomenon also occurs in Genesis in the Bible.

What do we think of a list of rulers before the Flood totalling 241,200 years (not 241,000) per the numbers given. Numbers of this size take us back close to the times of the earliest "big brained" fossil individual, the "Swanscombe" man's skull, unearthed in the 20th century, dated by archaeologists to about 250,000 years ago.

We might consider something else. The length of time from the Flood in the Sumerian God list to our present day is 31,359 years. This does not agree with our present estimates of when the last ice age ended, variously given as about 10 - 12,000 years ago. Apparently at the poles the last ice age ended about 1,000 years later than in the temperate zones.

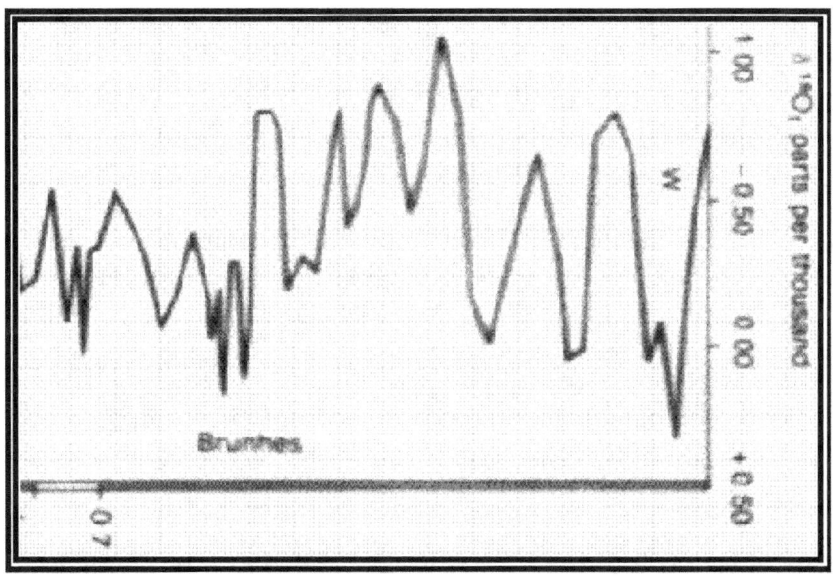

On the oxygen/isotope ice core table we find that from the datal point of 0.7 million years ago there are 68 x 1/16" to the present day on the scale. Therefore 1/16 inch represents approximately 10,000 years. If we measure the Sumerian 31,359 years as 3/16+ of an inch back from the present day on the table we find it gives us the lowest point in the entire table, which is just over 31,000 years ago.

If these measurements given in the table are accurate, there is here supporting evidence from a surprising source that something extraordinary indeed took place in the earth's history about 31,000+ years ago, which the Sumerians date as a Flood.

There may be another aspect to this picture of how our genealogy began -- provided by modern science and mitochondrial DNA or mtDNA. These are thought to be handed down by the mother alone. It should be possible to devise a 'clock' and track mt.genes back through the generations, provided the genetic material mutates at a constant rate, and that the mutations are not favoured or eliminated by natural selection. These are some very big "ifs" but a west coast U.S. group of scientists has calculated by such means that "Eve", or "the first modern man's mother,' probably lived between 100,000 and 150,000 years ago. These are fairly wide limits but another DNA 'clock' would suggest that Eve existed only 75,000 years ago.

What I find surprising from all this is that the ancient civilizations are giving us time scales not very different from these tentative datings by genetic and scientific dating methods. Until now prehistorians have dismissed these ancient "god lists" as pure myth -- many writers don't even trouble to mention them. I suggest this should change, and that the ancient writers' "god lists" should be taken more seriously.

It seems to me that the three civilizations we have mentioned, living so far apart and with very different languages: the Olmec, the Egyptian, and the Sumerian, are either copying one another, or more probably are each in their own way expressing their experience of the same type of event. That is, over long periods of time, first came the creation of domesticated plants and animals, then the creation of civilized man. And then much further back in time we have the phenomenon which the Sumerians called "kingship was lowered from heaven". This 272,500 year old event seems somehow to be connected in time with what we have found to be the appearance of a modern type of big-brained mankind, as distinct from ape-like creatures or hominids.

The Sumerians appear to have had no doubt as to what they meant by "kingship was lowered from heaven". They meant that their gods and goddesses, the Immortals, appeared and set up kingships on earth.

According to the ancient writers, it was these Immortals who domesticated plants and animals. The Immortals were aeons ahead of humans of their time in knowledge and brain power.

This takes us back to Alfred Wallace who you remember said that modern humans had something not derived from our animal progenitors - a spiritual essence or nature. Next we need to find out what ancient writers tell us about the so-called Immortals, in our effort to determine whether they really existed, if so, what part they played in the civilization process, and whether that infusion into humans is what caused the rapid creation of cities, civilizations and cultures at the end of the last ice age.

CHAPTER 14

THE ANCIENT WRITTEN RECORD

The people who lived about 5,300 years ago -- almost half way to the start of civilizations -- because that's what we're talking about -- these people, in Mesopotamia (which means between the two rivers) in what is now southern Iraq whose temples looked something like this:

and wrote on clay tablets like this:

had a complicated writing system that looked like this:

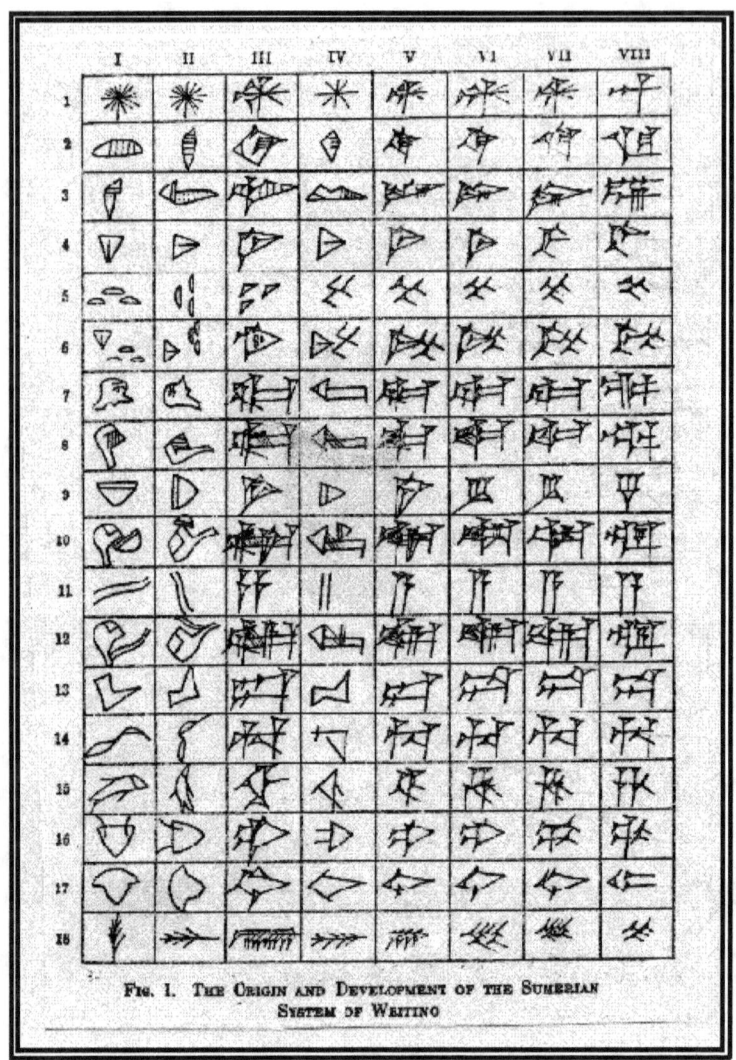

Fig. 1. The Origin and Development of the Sumerian System of Writing

and had a tradition of explaining how civilized man came into existence.

Because the tablets are so old and in such poor shape, the story has to be pieced together from various copies, some older than others. There are three main works of interest to us. The Enuma Elis ("When from on High" -- that's the opening of the first line) the Atra-hasis epic and the Gilgamesh Epic. Here's a shortened excerpt from the Atrahasis epic, to show you how poetic it was. To set the scene, we have the lesser gods and the greater gods. The lesser gods started the work of creating cities and irrigation schemes, then:

"When the gods, like men,
Bore the work and suffered the toil,
The toil of the gods was great
The work was heavy, the distress was much...
They were complaining, backbiting,
Grumbling in the excavation; They set fire to their tools,
Fire to their spades they put
And flame to their hods....
Nusku roused (his) lord,
He got him out of his bed,
'My lord (your) temple is surrounded,
Battle has come right up to your gate'."

Enlil...addressed the warrior Anu
'Summon one god and have him done to death.'

Anu opened his mouth
And addressed the gods, his brothers,
'What are we accusing them of?
Their work was heavy, their distress was much!"
While Belet-ili, the birth-goddess, is present...
Let her create Lullu--(man).
Let him bear the yoke asigned by Enlil
Let man carry the toil of the gods."

This is a very vivid and powerful style, from about 4,000 years ago or more. The unfamiliar names are all gods and goddesses, or the Immortals, as I call them, following the ancient Greek writer, Homer. The black-headed people is what the Sumerians called themselves.

Here we have reports involving intervention in human affairs by actual physically present gods and goddesses who were said by ancient writers to have taught human beings the complete arts and science of civilization. This has very little to do with the theory of evolution, where everything is said to have happened by a process of natural selection, competition and elimination over very long time periods to produce us as we are today as descendants from a tree shrew many millions of years ago.

Each of these "Immortals" owned their own "people" and territory and each was fed and waited on in his or her own "temple". The word 'temple' originally meant a house for a god or goddess and not a place of worship. Such an event would certainly explain the abrupt rise of civilizations, but how much can we rely on this ancient writers' evidence.

It's a vast subject, this frequent reference by ancient writers to intervention in human affairs by physically present gods and goddesses within the last 10,000 years. It could lead us across the Far East, the Near East, Egypt, North and South America, and that's what we'll look at in the next book in the series: The Immortals.

END

IS OUR

CIVILIZATION

DYING?

SECTION 1

This section contains an Introduction

and chapters 1 to 5

SECTION 2

This section contains chapters 6 to 10

SECTION 3

This section contains chapters 11 to 15

SECTION 1

INTRODUCTION

CHAPTER 1
WE INVENTED TIME:
CHANGE AND ORDER EXIST IN NATURE

CHAPTER 2
LIVING CELLS, SOCIETIES AND CIVILIZATIONS

CHAPTER 3
AN ISLAND CITY SOCIETY: VENICE

CHAPTER 4
DECLINE AND DEATH OF VENICE AS A SOCIETY

CHAPTER 5
CREATION OF LIVING SOCIETIES:
THE USA, RUSSIA, OTHERS

INTRODUCTION

Arnold Toynbee was interested in EF's views on civilizations and their societies when they met at Oxford. The result was that EF was granted a senior research fellowship at the University of Chicago which was the only place AT said he knew where he thought EF could research as he wanted to.

But it ended up with EF starting a study on the war of 1812. That was a long way from what EF had hoped for and was why he left the academic world to become a chartered accountant (equivalent of CPA in the US). Now, much later in life EF can write what he likes, and that's what's coming up in this part of the web site...

CHAPTER 1
WE INVENTED TIME:
CHANGE AND ORDER EXIST IN NATURE

Here's a city - it doesn't matter to us which one. We see from the air the Parkway is crowded, mostly with people going home from work. That's because it's 5 p.m. - what we call the time of day. But I suggest to you there's no such thing as time. The period it takes the earth to go round the sun we've divided into a year, months, days, hours, even hundredths of a second if you're an Olympic skier or nanoseconds if you're a scientist. But 'out there' what there is is change, different rates of change, and interaction between changing things to create more change. It's how successful a civilization is in adapting to change that determines whether or not it survives.

Let's vary our focus a bit. We're looking at the city as a whole now. There are millions of people down there but we can't see any of them. What we do see is traffic moving. We can see superhighways, the side streets, the residential areas neatly laid out, tall buildings near the centre, industrial areas and parks. It all looks very orderly.

This orderliness is important to us. If your TV screen shows 'snow' during a broadcast it's not chaos, a slight adjustment will bring back the picture, because the signal was there all the time. I suggest to you there's no such thing as chaos. Chaos is an order poorly understood, and disorder is part way between one set of order we can recognize, and another we can relate to. Water changes to ice to snow to steam and so on. But it never changes to iron. Why not? Because there's order, and that's why we can hope to understand how civilizations work; civilizations are orderly entities.

Let's move on to look down on another city. It doesn't seem very different. The traffic patterns are much the same. It has tall buildings near the centre, superhighways, residential areas neatly laid out, and so on. Agricultural products and raw materials flow in and technical services and manufactured goods flow out.

This second city is in the next door region to the first city but it doesn't allow signs with lettering the same size as signs in its own language to be put up in the language of the other city. That's just a minor example of the problems that have to be solved for a society to survive and prosper.

Both these cities are in the same country, or nation, which I've called a society. It's when you have cities in a society that there's a civilization. I suggest to you that without cities there is no civilization.

Cities tend to do business and exchange culture with one another. The major cities need smaller satellite cities and towns and rural areas in nearby regions to feed them. The major regional cities interact to form a society. Canada is a society. It's one society within a civilization. Western Civilization, we call it.

We are going to look at living in civilizations. But that's not the only way people on earth exist. Some are nomadic tribes-people. This doesn't mean they're 'uncivilized.' Often their standards of moral conduct, family co**hesion,** ability to survive, care for their environment, complexity of language and so on are far greater than that of many people living in cities. I would call them peripherals. They are outside present civilization, but may well form part of some future civilizations. Some have been part of arrested civilizations, not having settled down to agriculture and trading from a fixed location.

Today people mostly move about in vehicles propelled by volatile fuels using internal combustion engines. We use electric power to drive most equipment in our homes and offices. That's our technology.

Ancient Rome had horse drawn vehicles. There were bumps on their side roads to slow the chariots down, and posts in some roads to keep chariots out and leave a safe way for pedestrians. Downtown Rome once had a 70 ft. high building construction limit. They used water power, animal power and slave power to drive their mechanical equipment. They constructed aqueducts to carry clean water supplies to their cities for public baths and private use, and built coliseums for public entertainment activities. They made excellent long lasting straight roads. If we go back still further to ancient Egypt, ancient Mesopotamia, or ancient civilizations in Central and South America, we find tall buildings of a different kind from ours; stepped pyramids or ziggurats. So, each civilization has a different technology.

Wherever there are cities we have people specializing in doing certain work: architects, carpenters, doctors, engineers, law enforcement officers, lawyers, politicians, plumbers, priests, soldiers, teachers, and so on. There are people in these trades or professions whether it's ancient China, Greece or Rome, Egypt, South America, or today. Whatever the form of government, these trades and professions exist in every civilization we know of.

Societies within civilizations are more like plants in a field, or trees in a wood, than animals that can move about. A society is rooted in the land it finds itself in, and it lives or dies by its success in solving its problems where it is rooted. But societies grow and try to spread out, just as plants or trees do, and societies also colonize at a distance, just as plants and trees send out seeds to propagate at a distance. The Vikings reached England, Greenland, Iceland, Ireland, Labrador, Newfoundland, North Africa, down the Russian rivers as far as Kiev, and the U.S. east coast. Later, Portugal and Spain expanded overseas and the Pope divided the New World between them. Then England and France expanded overseas and competed in India and North America. Here we have important evidence that the nature of a society and a civilization includes the capacity to expand.

You'll have noticed we mentioned Portugal and Spain, England and France, and today we could add Russia and the USA, all within our civilization. We can go back to a previous civilization and notice Athens and Sparta, Carthage and Rome, and so on. The point is that they don't all spring up and expand at the same time like a crop in a field. Societies tend to flourish one after another, or two or three at a time.

Today, looking around us we can see that Portugal and Spain left their imprint on all of South America, and part of North America is Hispanic. But both Portugal and Spain shrank back to small societies. And since then Britain and France have shrunk back again. The societies we mentioned as being in a previous civilization are all extinct and when the last society ended the civilization passed away.

Some other societies have only recently begun to expand: Germany, Japan (an associate society to Western Civilization) and Russia. As the process is still going on in our civilization and societies within it are still rising and attempting to expand and assert themselves, apparently our Western Civilization has some way to go before it becomes naturally extinct.

What are the limits of a civilization? I think much broader than we've generally thought. The ancient Egyptian, Greek, Mesopotamian, Phoenician, and Roman existences I suggest we include in one civilization. They fought, traded, recognized one another's gods and goddesses, and their rulers intermarried. Let's call it the Mediterranean Civilization.

All these ancient societies and their civilization itself are long since dead. So are other old civilizations in India, China, South America, Central America. So if they're dead, how long did they live? And why did they die?

We can only ask that kind of question and expect an answer if we look at societies and civilizations as living entities in themselves and forget about the individuals in them, just as we did when we looked at a city from the air. Then we were not aware of individuals being born and dying in the city though all that was going on as we looked. In the same way we're not aware of many different kinds of individual cells in our bodies coming into existence and later dying, yet it goes on all the time within us. As long as we think of a society as a collection of individuals with special individual leaders we know of by name, we're not going to understand a society properly. We have to acknowledge a society is a living entity. I suggest to you that's just what it is.

CHAPTER 2

LIVING CELLS, SOCIETIES AND CIVILIZATIONS

Human beings create and maintain societies and civilizations. What are humans actually made of? Basically, according to our present state of knowledge, cells. There are far more living cells in your one body than there are people on this planet. There are about 60,000 miles in your circulatory system. The blood coursing through your major veins and arteries is a continuous movement of cells, something like the traffic in our cities, except that in the body, traffic is all one way and so more efficient. You don't have half the width of a vein with not much traffic and the other half clogged in a rush hour. Our governments, large industries, schools, universities, offices, banks and stock exchanges are centres of activity, as are the major organs in our bodies: heart, liver, stomach, brain, lungs, and so on. There are said to be one hundred thousand million atoms in a single cell. Cells in us are like people in a society.

There are said to be from 210 to 411 different kinds of cells in the human body and about 100 trillion, yes, trillion, altogether. When we look at an individual cell, although we need a microscope to see it, we find it's not a simple thing. It's more like a factory. Things pass in and out of its walls, some things are excluded, others are not. Vast numbers of chemical reactions take place inside it with lightning speed. There are various complicated parts and structures inside the cell. Eukaryotic cells have organelles that live and reproduce and multiply within them. The organelles perform chemical work inside the cell and have their own double helix of DNA inside them completely separate and containing different information from the DNA in the cell nucleus. How does a cell become a liver cell, or a stomach cell? We're told it knows where its place is. It certainly knows what to do.

These billions of cells cooperate within us to do their work. We don't know exactly how or why they do this, but if they didn't work together, if they went on strike, we'd quickly die. We've never met any of these cells as individuals, we've never talked to them. We live in worlds of different dimensions, but they are somehow us. Each of your cells is a distinct individual with its own life within you. And your cells live out their lives together inside you, forming you.

A society doesn't have much interest in individual people. It taxes them, governs them, punishes them, educates them, transports them, gives them recreational facilities, health care, and so on. But people are faceless multitudes to the society. We are just the same with the cells in our bodies. We feed them, take in air and water for them, keep their habitat clean and so on, but we don't know them, though they live and die and reproduce in us, even for us. In a sense they are us, but we're not conscious of them.

A cell seems to be programmed by its DNA code, something 6 feet long rolled up inside it. The DNA in the single cell apparently has the code to reproduce the whole individual person, and an individual civilized person has the ability to start the creation of a whole society. But when we, as individuals, try to understand a civilization it's rather like a single cell of the billions in our body trying to understand how the whole human being operates.

. . . .

We shouldn't overestimate our own knowledge in our day and age. Our scientists say the sun is a nuclear furnace. They tell us the universe began with a small very dense ball which exploded with a big bang. Don't you think it's significant that the age that has discovered nuclear power and invented the hydrogen bomb should now interpret the universe in terms of that technology. When technology advances again we'll be sure to have new explanations of the solar system and the universe in terms of that technology. So when we come to look at civilizations we have to be able to stand outside all these ideas and thought patterns and see them for what they are; products of their age.

If we want comparisons with past societies and civilizations we have to rely mostly on historians and archaeologists for our raw material. That presents a problem. For example, it's been said that if we had to rely on archaeology alone, we would never have known there was a Norman conquest of England. But that event was a monumental change in the course of the history of the English society.

A further example: what we are being told by some scholars (who are themselves the product of our age) is that about 3,000 to 3,500 years ago Stone Age people in South America had implements that were fancy stone clubs used for warfare and religious ceremonies. That conforms with our general ideas about Stone Age people. Since Darwin and Wallace the view of history has been that it is a linear progression from Stone Age cave dwellers to the present. What I'm suggesting (see my The Walls of Cyclops) is that people in South America were using the same technical principles as we do today in similar ore bodies, and that about 3,000 to 3,500 years ago they were drilling for gold, silver and copper which was used for ornaments, housewares, and so on. I believe I am on firm ground in this case because as a chartered accountant one of my clients was a manufacturer of deep rock drilling equipment.

This wasn't the only Stone Age phenomenon. Look at Stonehenge, first built even earlier. A generation ago conventional wisdom held that Stonehenge was connected with the invading Beaker People. Recently the prevailing view seems to be that probably there weren't any invading Beaker People. We still don't know who the people were who built Stonehenge, or what they used it for. What we do know is that there were thousands of stone circles in Europe in that Age, stretching from what is now Turkey to what is now Scotland. There are astronomical alignments at Stonehenge, and we don't know why. (see my The Mysterious Cursus). Stonehenge has its great stone uprights weighing 45 tons shaped with what architects today call entasis: the uprights have slightly convex tapering to counteract the optical illusion of curving slightly inward when seen from a distance. The tops were slightly 'dished' to carry the 7 ton lintels and the lintels and uprights were further secured by mortice and tenon joints. Some of the most massive blocks of stone in ancient Egypt were used to create the oldest structures; the Osirion, a beautiful rectangular pool and courtyard dressed in stone and surrounded by huge blocks of finished stone, and a building with massive blocks of stone now said to have been a temple.

I would call this Age of technical mastery in stone the Stone Civilization. That particular civilization began with agriculture, wood products, and stone implements and moved on to massive stone block construction and use of copper for implements. We know next to nothing about this civilization except for a few of its architectural remains.

The Mediterranean Civilization (discussed in chapter 1) began with city states using stone and copper but moved to bricks and bronze, and ended with empires using roads, aqueducts, fleets of wooden ships, concrete and iron. We know quite a lot about this civilization although some of it is poorly understood. Our present Western Civilization, which is still going on, began with know-how in stone, iron, bricks and concrete, and so on, and has moved through the Industrial Age to the Space Age with electric, internal combustion and nuclear power. The other two civilizations are dead.

We don't have many examples of civilizations to work on. The very beginning of civilizations seems to have been about 10,000 years ago, unless some earlier ones were drowned at the end of the last ice age. Many societies have come and gone, but very few civilizations. There's been some accumulation of knowledge. We still use bricks, and we use the running bond pattern for bricklaying, just as the ancient Mesopotamians did about 5,000 years ago in a different civilization. But a lot gets left behind and forgotten between civilizations that have 'dark ages' or relatively uncivilized periods between them, even though the intelligence of individuals may have continued without interruption.

Has human intelligence or moral sense improved during the last few thousand years? Do we today really have more brains or morality than Aristotle, Euclid, Pythagoras or Archimedes? Do we have better laws than those of Hammurabi or the Ten Commandments? Can we tell a better tale than Homer? I suggest to you that human intelligence and morality haven't improved significantly since the beginnings of civilizations.
. . . .

I think we have to recognize 3 different things here: an age, a technology, and a civilization. At more or less the same time, civilizations around the world, in China, Europe, India, Central and South America, for example, were using similar technology: animal power, water power, people power, and stone or copper or bronze. That's because societies are great imitators. No one can get too far ahead for long.

We can see how the technological change from the Industrial Age to the present Space Age is affecting us as individual people and our culture in our own time. I think there's a recognizable pattern here, but as it's civilizations we're dealing with the span is very broad and the cycle is very long. We have to reckon in thousands of years. And since we've moved from the Industrial to the Space Age without our civilization dying we know for a fact that a civilization has more than one Age in its life cycle.
. . . .

Difficult as it is for us to stand back and try to understand a civilization this must be our next step. I suggest the best way to do this is to start with one specimen from a civilization, a single society. I think the simplest type is what I would call an Island City Society. There have been quite a few of them, including Tyre, and Tyre's colony, Carthage, in the dead Mediterranean civilization. But that's not our civilization and we don't know enough about those cities. We don't even know when Tyre was founded. Then there are living Island City Societies, such as Singapore and Hong Kong. They're still quite young. Hong Kong started in 1841 AD, so it's only about 160 years old and incomplete. Hong Kong may come to an unnatural end by having been absorbed into China in the late 1990s, or it may have the energy with its 6 million people to change China itself with its billion plus people. It's too early to see how the change will develop.

Not all societies live to die a natural death. Tyre was murdered by Alexander the Great. It took him about seven months to do it. Before he could capture the city he built a causeway to reach the island and set up 2000 crosses within sight of the city walls, ready for crucifying the nobler citizens. After the bloodbath when the city fell he sold most of the survivors into slavery.

We need as our first example an Island City Society that lived and died in our own Western civilization. We need direct evidence we can use as well as having to rely on what historians tell us. It's not history we're after, but evidence for the life pattern of a society. Then we can apply this pattern to the incomplete societies around us today and have a better idea of how to prepare for the future. I think there is such an Island City Society for us to look at: it began as marsh and island flats, rose to be a world power, and then declined into just a city, and is now gradually physically becoming submerged as sea levels rise around the world. It's Venice, and next we'll look at its life cycle.

CHAPTER 3

AN ISLAND CITY SOCIETY: VENICE

We know exactly how Venice began - with urban refugees after the sack of Rome and its nearby northern satellite cities. Some of these people fled to the 117 mud flat islands, sand banks, and lagoons which later grew to be Venice. It was impossible to get at them there and their possessions weren't worth looting anyway.

We know exactly when Venice began, 421 AD on 25th of March. We know exactly when Venice ceased to exist as an Island City State: Napoleon, who said with a sense of history 'I shall be Attila for the State of Venice', declared war on Venice on May 1, 1797. The government collapsed and the ruler, the Doge, abdicated. Then, without a fight, Napoleon stripped it of its wealth and it became just another Italian city. So the life span of Venice as an Island City Society was 1,376 years.

Just to test this life span, we can take two other societies that we know about; Rome itself was founded, so legend has it, in 753 BCE (before Christian era) and was sacked by the Visigoths in 410 AD. Actually its power had become so vast it was sacked more than once and it took 66 more years to finally destroy it. So its life span was 1,229 years. Byzantium was intended as the eastern Roman empire, but in fact became a separate state. Its capital was founded in 326 AD by Constantine; that's why it was called Constantinople. It was besieged and overwhelmed by the Turks and sacked in 1453 AD. That time span is 1,127 years. This gives us some idea of the scale of the life cycle of a society. All three were killed off while rotting away in old age, just as elderly humans are killed off, by influenza, for example.

Carthage was unlucky enough to be a contemporary society with Rome. It had 3 Punic wars with Rome, lasting 23 years, 17 years, and the final war only 3 years. In the second,

Hannibal marched his army from Spain across the Pyrenees, crossed the Rhone river, crossed through the Alps into Italy, apparently elephants included - the living tanks of the day. He smashed every Roman army he met, and then was let alone to move about in Italy until the Carthaginians grew tired of voting troops and money to him, and he left. He never did attack the city of Rome. Later, Scipio, a young Roman general, defeated him near Carthage in 202 BCE. In 146 BCE the fleet of 500 ships was towed out to sea and sunk, the citizens massacred or sold as slaves, the city was stripped, the buildings torn down, the site ploughed up and a curse put on it. Said to have been founded about 653 BCE, it was put to death after only 507 years.

Now let's look a little closer at the life span of Venice. It began by building up its site, it developed a local monopoly in salt, very important in the days before refrigeration; our word salary comes from the Latin word for salt as the Romans gave an allowance to each soldier. The early Venetians learned boat building and ship handling. The various lagoon populations joined together, the people assembled to decide matters of state, and after 140 years the 12 main islands elected 12 tribunes. About another 130 years after that they elected their first communal ruler, or Doge.

Venice survived the ravages on the nearby mainland of the Visigoths, the Huns, the Vandals, and then the Franks. When Charlemagne led the Franks, in about 800 AD he executed 4,500 Saxons in one day. This at a time when populations around the world were very small by our standards. In 1378 AD the population of London is said to have been only about 46,000. Charlemagne and his father before him tried to conquer Venice but failed.

Byzantium gradually conquered a fair part of the old western Roman Empire. Venice began to act as its western maritime outpost. It transported generals and supplies for Byzantium. When Charlemagne finally made peace with Byzantium a Venetian official was present and the existence of Venice was formally acknowledged. In recognition of its services Byzantium gave Venice trading privileges throughout its empire. It's said that Charlemagne always wore a Venetian tunic. So, after about 400 years of life Venice had developed maritime ability, was a trading state in luxury goods between east and west and a unified well organized society.

We don't know much about those first 400 years of Venice, but we know much more about the beginnings of Hong Kong. Both have the characteristic growth pattern of an Island City Society so let's turn to Hong Kong now. In the 1830s AD Hong Kong was a group of 236 islands with a population of about 5,000, said to be mostly stone cutters, fishermen, smugglers and pirates. British merchants had been ordered out of Canton by the government of China. Britain went to war with China over this and in the peace that followed received a lease on Hong Kong; 90% of it expired in 1997. The emperor is said to have laughed when the British wanted it. But Hong Kong has one of the largest, finest natural harbours in the world. Ocean going ships couldn't reach Canton, so Hong Kong became its port, with the displaced British merchants. That was in 1841.

In the 1940s Hong Kong survived being overrun by the Japanese. In the 1990s the Chinese (formerly mainland) population was about 98% of the total population of about 6 million. It has shipbuilding, low cost industrial technology and electronic 'high tec'. It is a free port and so has become an international trading centre. Yet, like Venice, it is incapable of supporting itself from its own territory.

Both Venice and Hong Kong suffer from site over-population. In the 1930s Venice had only 6,000 of 19,000 homes with any form of sewage arrangement. Over the centuries the houses have collected rainwater for drinking and flushed raw sewage out into the canals. Goethe complained about the filth 200 years ago. A slight tide helps wash most of it away into the Adriatic.

Before 1997 Hong Kong had a Governor and Legislative Council. That's not very different from the Doge and 12 Tribunes set up by Venice. The main point seems to be that an international trading centre needs only enough government to maintain order, and basically to be left alone and not overtaxed. Hong Kong began by being sheltered under the British Empire and Venice by being sheltered under the Byzantine Empire. Hong Kong began as an open door between the West and China. Venice built up its power by trading in luxury goods between east and west, spices, silks, and so on, and used an up-dated version of the Roman galleys. The galleys had a crew of about 200 and each man was an entrepreneur who could take goods stowed under his rowing bench and trade on his own account. The galleys were fast, safer from pirates, and avoided the tolls levied on overland caravans. Venice was a ship builder. Hong Kong is a ship builder.

We need to look outside Venice now to better understand how and why it prospered so well. Mohammed died in 632 AD when Venice was about 200 years old. After Mohammed there came a remarkable expansion among the converts to Islam: the Arabs and the Turks. The Arabs spread the faith across north Africa. They eventually crossed the straits of Gibraltar and entered Europe through their attacks on Spain. The Turks began pushing towards Europe from the eastern end and across the Dardanelles which meant they met Byzantium head on. It took them about 1,000 years but eventually they conquered the Balkans, Hungary, besieged Vienna, capital of Austria, and declared war on Russia. That was as far as they got in Europe. Bismarck, German Chancellor in the late 1800s could call Turkey the 'sick man of Europe', about 1,240 years after the rise of Islam in Turkey.

The Seljuks - one branch of the Turks - took Jerusalem in 1,071. Before 1,100 the first Crusade was organized by the North Atlantic and Central European powers to take it back. They needed Venetian support as experts in the area. In exchange they gave Venice trading rights in their own states and Venice helped them take Askelon, Tyre and Acre. Venice received 1/4 of Acre, and a street in every city of the kingdom of Jerusalem, with a bakery, public bath, market, and church. The Venetians didn't have to pay any taxes and their goods paid no duties. Venice sacked and pillaged Rhodes where the best looking youths of both sexes were sold as slaves and the plunder was described as the most fabulous since creation. Venice, with its fleet of galleys, was also helping Byzantium against the Turks and was rewarded with trading privileges there.

About 750 years after its beginnings, Venice, this city of 150,000, was said to have a colony of 200,000 merchants and others in Constantinople, capital of Byzantium. They were so rowdy and arrogant that their goods were confiscated and their trading privileges cancelled. But the Turks kept pressing on the Byzantines who by 17 years later, needing the help of Venice, restored all Venetian privileges with compensation.

Now we come to the real turning point in the life cycle of Venice - the 4th Crusade (1,202). Venice was not quite 800 years old at the time. The Northern powers wanted Venice to transport them to the Holy Land. They even collected at Venice. They had 4,500 horses, 9,000 knights, 20,000 foot soldiers and provisions for 1 year. Venice put the price at 85,000 marks, cash in advance. My calculation is that this would be about $103,445,000 today. The crusaders didn't have cash, so Venice bargained with them to stop on the way to the Holy Land and put down a local insurrection in the colony of Venice on the Dalmatian coast, and this was done.

Next, Venice wasn't too pleased with Byzantium for cutting off its trading privileges, even temporarily. The Crusaders had with them the son of the former Byzantine emperor who had been deposed and blinded. The Crusaders and Venice agreed to sack Constantinople, a Christian capital. Venice took fabulous spoils as well as architects, craftsmen, artists, and secured Byzantine overseas possessions - the Cyclades, the Sporades, the islands and eastern shore of the Adriatic, the shores of the Propontis and the Euxine and the littoral of Thessaly, and Venice bought Crete.

Venice now controlled the Adriatic, the Ionian Islands, the archipelago, the sea of Marmora and the Black sea, the trade route between Constantinople and western Europe and was established in the sea ports of Syria. Of the 12 electors who set up the new emperor of Byzantium 6 were controlled by Venice. Venice was now a world power.

Here's part of the Doge's "State of the Nation" address when Venice was at the height of its power, just over 1,000 years from its beginning:

"My Lords,... In my time 4 millions of debts have been paid off, and there are other 6 millions owing, which debt was incurred for the wars of Padua, Vicenza, and Verona; we have paid every 6 months 2 instalments of the debts, and have paid all my officers and regiments. This our city now sends out in the way of business to different parts of the world 10 million ducats' worth yearly by ships and galleys, and the profit is not less than 2 million ducats a year. In this city there are 3,000 vessels of one to 200 'enfore' (measure of capacity) with 17,000 seamen; there are 300 larger ships with 8,000 sailors. Every year there go to sea 45 galleys with 11,000 sailors, and there are 3,000 ship's carpenters and 3,000 caulkers. There are 3,000 weavers of silk and 16,000 weavers of cotton cloth; the houses are estimated to be worth 7,050,000 ducats. The rents are 500,000 ducats. There are 1,000 noblemen whose income is from 700 to 4,000 ducats. If you go on in this manner you will increase from good to better, and you will be the masters of wealth and Christendom; everyone will fear you. But beware, as you would be of fire, of taking what belongs to others and of waging unjust war, for God cannot

endure those errors in princes. Everyone knows that the war with the Turks has made you brave and experienced of the sea, you have 6 generals fit to fight any great army, and for each of these you have sea captains... officers... and rowers enough to man 100 galleys; and in these years you have
shown distinctly that the world considers you the leaders of Christianity. You have many doctors of diverse sciences, and especially lawyers wherefore numerous foreigners come here for judgement of their differences and abide by your verdicts.
Your mint coins every year a million ducats of gold and
200,000 of silver... Therefore be wise in governing such a State and be careful to watch it and see that it is not diminished by negligence..."

By my calculations, translating the Doge's information into modern statistics, Venice had a GNP (gross national product) of over $26 billion and controlled a population of probably over 20 million, which is greater than the present population of Australia, or Austria, or Bolivia, Cambodia, Chile, Ecuador, Hungary, Iraq... and so on.

The Venetians whose income was 4,000 ducats yearly would have more than $10 million annually today.

Incidentally, Marco Polo, a Venetian, left in 1271 and travelled overland to China where he spent 17 years including service with Kublai Khan, before returning to Venice. He was impressed with China's wealth and power. The wealthy Venetians response to his stories was "Oh, really?" "Yeah?" "You don't say" ...

At this stage we're just looking at some of the more important information about the life cycle of Venice as an Island City Society. When we've followed it to its end, - which we'll do in the next chapter - we can deduce a pattern and begin to apply it to others to see if there's a resemblance. Then we can better understand where we're at today which is something history doesn't tell us.

CHAPTER 4

DECLINE AND DEATH OF VENICE AS A SOCIETY

We left Venice at about 800 years old, when it had just become a world power, which it was by 1220 AD. As early as the 1200s double entry bookkeeping, the basis of modern accounting systems, was brought into use at the Rialto, the Venetian commercial centre and clearing house. It may be that the ancient Romans knew the principle of the system, Suitonius writing in about 110 AD mentions 'the debit side of the ledger', but the Venetians brought it into modern practical business and so provided themselves with accurate and efficient record keeping.

For about 800 years this city of 150,000 had a virtual monopoly of the luxury trade from east to west. But Venice in its rise to power had bitten off the hand that fed it: Byzantium. It cannibalized that society just as Rome had done earlier with Carthage and other societies, including Egypt. By weakening Byzantium, Venice inherited its problem: expansion of the Turks.

Venice, on the east side of Italy, also faced the bitter rivalry of Genoa on Italy's west side. Venice and Genoa fought intermittently for about 150 years, with first one side winning, and then the other. They fought several sea battles. Finally Venice won a 3 year war. From then on Genoa ceased to be a significant naval power.

Even before the final victory over Genoa, Venice was fighting Hungary over the Dalmatian coast. And while that intermittent fighting was going on, Venice began fighting inland in northern Italy. One by one it took over the smaller towns in its area: Verona, Vicenza, Fruili, Brescia, Bergamo, Ravenna, Crema, Treviglio, the Polesimo, and so on. This drew the attention of France and Spain who had been trying to partition up Italy between them.

In 1509 the League of Cambrai had France, Spain, the Holy Roman Empire, the Pope and even Henry 8th of England together against Venice which lost the war and all its mainland possessions. But Venetian diplomacy helped the victors to quarrel and within a year or two Venice had most of it back, but it cost 5 million ducats. Some have argued this started the decline of Venice, now about 1,100 years old. But most of the Italian 'terrafirma' was glad to have back the enlightened rule of Venice, which held much of it until the time of Napoleon.

Probably Venice could have remained a much larger player in Europe had it been able to take over all the major Renaissance cities in northern Italy: Florence, Genoa, Mantua, Milan, Padua and Pisa. But intermittently Venice was fighting the Turks in the east at the same time. It's said that Venice attacked the Italian mainland because the small states there were charging excessive tolls and levies on Venetian imports going to Germany and northern Europe. But Venice was also running out of room on its islands, it constantly needed more lumber for shipbuilding, as it suffered losses in war and wooden ships only last a few years anyway. The wealthy citizens needed room to relax on shore and set up larger industries there with less water and sanitation problems.

After the Turks had finished off Byzantium by capturing Constantinople, Venice traded with them such as by importing Turkish rugs, and made treaties with the Turks when it could. But even before 1500 Venice found it necessary to cede Albania and Lemnos to the Turks and pay a tribute of 100,000 ducats for the retention of trading privileges. At the end of the next war with the Turks it had to offer 6,000 ducats for Malvasia and 300,000 as indemnity for the war. This was rejected and the Venetians had to give up some Dalmatian ports as well. Eventually Crete, which Venice had held for 450 years, was captured by the Turks after a 24 year war in which the heroic Venetian commander was captured, flayed alive, his skin stuffed and put on display in the Turkish capital. By 1718, within 100 years of the end, all major overseas possessions were lost.

In the early days the council met every day of the week including Sundays and every holiday except 2 in the year. In summer they sat from 8 to 12 and in winter from noon to sunset. Some of the older nobles had hardly missed a day in 30 or 40 years of service. Then the "Golden Book" of the noble families was closed. An ingrowing aristocracy resulted.

Between about 1200 and 1700 when Venice was between 800 and 1300 years old, Venice fought about 50 wars. Many of the best men were gradually killed off, Venice resorted to mercenaries, (as Carthage had done); massive debts piled up to finance the wars. Then titles were offered for sale - 100,000 ducats would buy one - official positions were for sale, and Venice became exhausted militarily and in spirit.

Venice did adapt when it could. It even partially recovered the spice trade threatened by Portugal after discovery of the Cape route to the East Indies. There was a further blow to Venice in the sailing ship revolution. Ocean going round-hulled merchant ships with guns and gunpowder could more or less defend themselves with a small crew while 200 man galleys were expensive to crew and not suited to ocean-going trade.

At its peak the Venetian state-owned ship-building yard, the Arsenal, employed 16,000 men and by assembly line methods could build a ship a day. They gave a practical demonstration for Henry 3rd of France who visited Venice in 1574 and saw a galley put together in a few hours.

As the local supplies of lumber were used up, the Venetian merchants were prepared to ship goods in foreign vessels or have ships built on the Dalmatian coast, or at Ragusa, which became a colonial competitor. But the Venetian government put duties and tariffs on foreign shipping, so that considerable trade shifted to Leghorn and Ragusa, to the disadvantage of Venetian entrepreneurs.

Now that its eastern monopoly was declining, Venetian ingenuity turned to industry. Venice developed a fine quality woollen trade, and the highest quality glass, mirrors, and lacquered furniture. Even today we have Venetian blinds as quality adjustable shades for windows (but not made in Venice). The English and the Dutch were more experienced ocean going navigators - they lived next to oceans and had adapted to them in their development. They sailed right through the Mediterranean to trade with Turkey. England took 40% of the Aleppo trade and left Venice only 25%. Worse, English and Flemish manufacturers were taking their cheap imitations of Venetian quality goods to the eastern Mediterranean. (Britain had the same complaint about Germany in the late 1800s and North America about the Pacific Rim States in the late 1900s).

When Venice was about 1000 years old its arts began to flourish. Genoa produced Columbus, Florence produced Boccacio, Dante, Machiavelli, the Medicis, Michelangelo, and Leonardo. From Pisa came Galileo. Venice produced Bellini, Cabot (a naturalized Venetian), Canaletto, El Greco, Gabrieli, Marco Polo, Monteverdi (concert master there), Spinetus (who invented the spinet), Tintoretto, and Vivaldi. Except for Marco Polo, who was earlier, all this took place when Venice was between 1000 and 1300 years old.

During the final 150 years everything fell apart; but the reasons for it lay mostly in the 140 years or so before that, so let's look at that period first - from about 1505 to 1645 if you like historical dates.

In 1505 Venice was almost 1100 years old. Its colonies were competing with it, producing more cheaply than it could. Soon after its defeat by the League of Cambrai in 1509, a new experience in its lifetime, it joined the Pope, Spain, and Henry 8th's England against France which was invading Italy. Then 13 years later Venice joined the Pope, France, Florence, and Milan against the Holy Roman Empire.

Venice had been warring against the Turks on and off all this time and was instrumental in defeating Turkish sea power at Lepanto in 1571. But the Turks took Cyprus from Venice. All these wars were very costly to Venice. And during this period there was European inflation. But while English builders' wages went up 25%, the Venetian increase was 100%. Volunteer oarsmen were being replaced by convicts. France switched its importing from Venice to its own Marseilles, and the English traded direct with the near east or through Leghorn.

We can see why: Venetian taxes were too high, labour costs were too high, workers were becoming inefficient, there were high city wages for services, sites were expensive, there were frustrating guild (labour union) restrictions. The government tried to curb wage increases but found it impossible. Let's take an example. Around 1600 AD Venetian cloth was of the highest quality. An average 'piece' cost 79 ducats. The average components were:

Government taxes 33 ducats (42%)
Labour costs . . . . 34 ducats (43%)
Merchant's share 12 ducats (15%)
Total 79

From that 12 ducats or 15% the merchant had to provide for the raw material cost (probably at least 10%); overhead (probably about 10% today); a return on capital to investors (which should be at least 5%); a reserve for replacements and improvements (say 5%) and then 'profits' **or** wages of the merchant, (which should be at least 5%).

You can see that the money isn't there, and the product was already over-priced in the world market. The taxes were high because the wars were killing Venice. Venice was now in a world class league without a monopoly any more to support it.

Now let's look at the last 140 to 150 years when Venice was over 1200 years old. Everything began unravelling. First, a 24 year war to the death to defend Crete against the Turks. The cost far exceeded the 5 million ducats annually in taxation.
Every Venetian had to give up 3/4 of his family plate to be melted down. The taxes rose higher than ever. The government debt rose to 80 million ducats and required annual interest payments of 2.5 million ducats.

No wonder that the cloth tenderers' guild had 22 masters and 12 unemployed, and the tanners with 63 in the guild had 35 unemployed (before 1700 AD). There were less than 2000 beggars in the 1500s AD but over 20,000 in the late 1600s. Many skilled workers moved to other parts of Europe.

Public morals disintegrated. An abbess and a nun fought with daggers over a lover. A woman put up her daughter's virginity as a lottery prize. Someone prepared a book listing over 11,600 call girls. Casinos sprang up everywhere.

The Arsenal, which once employed over 16,000 now had about 1,500 men. 70,000 pieces of lumber intended for shipbuilding disappeared annually, used by workers to heat their homes. Many workers had other jobs and only turned up for payday. Apprentices in the guilds paid for their certificates instead of working for them. Government offices were for sale.
The army cost as much as ever but was corrupt. Corfu should have been defended by 1 company of Venetians and 2 of Albanians. In fact there were only a couple of Venetian officers who drew the pay for the lot. Colonial defences were decayed. Guns were rusted up or without ammunition. Battlements were overgrown with bushes and trees.

The cost of the 19 day election campaign for the Doge was about 70,000 lire around 1700 AD and about 400,000 lire just before the end. Within 20 years of the end the Doge had said "We have no forces, on land or sea. We have no alliances. We live by luck, by chance." It was a pathetic ending, in 1797. Just after an ultimatum from Napoleon about a new form of government was read in the Great Council, there was a discharge of musketry outside. In panic the members voted 513 yeas, 30 nays, and 5 blanks. Then, having signed themselves out of office, they went home.

But the musket shots weren't the French troops after all. They were the parting salute of the Slavonic troops, the mercenary palace guard, leaving because the French minister had said they 'irritated' him and so the Venetian government had ordered them to leave. Then Napoleon, without a fight, began the systematic looting of the treasures of Venice. The crown jewels were removed, precious metals melted down, the finest art catalogued and shipped to the Louvre in Paris. So ended Venice, the Island City Society which lasted from the sack of the Roman Empire to the looting of Venice by Napoleon, 1376 years.

The peninsula of Italy was a patchwork of small states at the time. But soon afterwards Cavour and Garibaldi were among the leaders of the 'risorgimento' or resurrection of the Italian spirit of the Renaissance and even of ancient Rome, leading to the unification of Italy. By 1861 King Victor Emmanuel 2nd, king of Sardinia, was able to proclaim himself king of Italy and in 1866 Venetia was finally wrested from the Austrians for Italy. In less than 90 years after its end as a distinct Society, Venice was swallowed up with its competitors into a new, much larger entity, a Nation State.

CHAPTER 5

CREATION OF LIVING SOCIETIES:

THE USA, RUSSIA, OTHERS

Remembering that our example of Venice was just one type of society, an Island City Society, which had a simplistic beginning, now we're ready to test the theory on some of the societies that are important to us in our present Western Civilization: alphabetically, Britain, Canada, France, Germany, Russia, and the United States of America.

First, we have to know when they started. This is where a lot of people have given up. It all looks like an endless stream of history to them. But if I'm right in saying societies are living entities and have life cycles then there has to be a start. So, what are we looking for? I think it's:

1. A precise location. We've seen that societies don't move around, they're rooted. They take their chances where they began, like trees. So they should have begun where they are today.
2. The name should be the same. It's true Venice was briefly called Rivo Alto at the beginning but it soon became Venice and kept that name. So the earliest use of the present name will be of help to us
.

3. We want continuity. If a society dies out early on, then that's not a full life and we're talking about life cycles. If it ceases, like Gilbert's colony in Newfoundland, or the lost colony of Roanoke in Virginia, then we have to look for a different start.
Later on we'll look for the characteristic phases: formative, ascendancy, expansion with cannibalism, dominance, decay, and termination or death. Right now we'll concentrate on starts. Let's take the easy ones first.

CANADA

The name Canada came from the Huron-Iroquois language kanata (settlement) as told to and used by Jacques Cartier in 1535. By 1550 it was already being shown on European maps as the name for part of present eastern Canada.

We know when Canada started as our present Canada, because we know from looking at Venice that it has to be started by people from another society within a civilization. The first permanent settlement of that kind was in 1604 when Acadia was founded.

THE USA

The name America came from a German map maker who read the popular accounts of the travels of Florentine merchant Amerigo Vespucci and named the territory after him in 1507.

The US generally regards its beginning as the 1607 settlement in Virginia. But Spain's American empire began with Cortez in Mexico from 1520, De Soto along the Mississippi from 1539, Coronado beyond the Rio Grande and Menendez who founded the first European settlement in North America, in Florida in 1565. Then came the French with forts along the Ohio river, La Salle on the Mississippi to the gulf of Mexico, calling it Louisiana, founding New Orleans at the mouth of the river. As late as 1701 La Salle founded Detroit for France. There were also Dutch and Swedish colonies. So here we have complications. What is the true beginning of the US? I think we have to give recognition to the various influences, particularly the Spanish, as the US took New Mexico, Texas, and California from Mexico. So do we take 1520 as the start of what eventually became part of the US, or 1565, as the first European permanent settlement, or the first permanent English settlement, in Virginia in 1607, as the area that motivated the existence of the society that is the US?

From our point of view, dealing with societies with long life spans, we don't care much which date is used. We're looking at change in status of the territory which was to become the US. We could just as well say 1520, as 1607, because we're not trying to be historians here, we're after something different. But the US, unlike Mexico, is fundamentally English speaking, although Spanish is increasingly a second language, so let's say it started in 1607.

. . . .

If we had slight problems finding the start of the US, where do we begin with Britain, France, Germany, and Russia? It may not be as hopeless as you might think. Let's take Britain next.

BRITAIN
We know that just before the Roman society died, Roman legions started moving out of Britain, and the last of them left by 409 AD. After they left, the Roman colonial society in Britain collapsed and died. So we know there has to be a fresh start, a new society has to come into existence after that. But the Romans hadn't even left before the Picts, Irish, and Saxons were already invading Britain. Then came the Angles, and Jutes. Three small kingdoms took shape, Northumbria, in the north, Mercia in the west, and Wessex in the south and east. Offa, king of Mercia, built a 'dyke' to keep out the Welsh, and subdued just about everyone else, except the Danes and Vikings who were starting to come in. But the first king to call himself King of the English was Egbert of Wessex in 802. Both Mercia and Northumbria did homage to him. Several other kings followed Egbert, then came Alfred 'the Great'.

Britain was really founded as an independent society during the reign of Alfred (871 - 900 AD). He was a successful warrior, organized a navy, re-organized the army, was an educated man himself, invited scholars to his court, founded schools, churches and monasteries, patronized merchants and explorers, and was a great law-giver.

Alfred's successor Edmund the Elder was acknowledged as king or as overlord over the whole island. Athelstan (925 - 940) became lord of the whole of Britain:

"Rex Anglorum curegulus totius Britanniae"

If we look forward a few years we find the Danes took over half the country, and later, one of them, Canute, became king of England. Then Harold Hardrada of Norway attacked and was defeated by Harold king of England in the north in 1066, a few weeks before William of Normandy landed in the south. Harold marched his army south and chose to meet William's forces without delay. He was killed and his army defeated at Hastings on the south coast.

So England, which later grew to be Britain, started somewhere in there. Do we take 802 or 871 as our starting date? The title came into existence with Egbert, but the reality began to take shape with Alfred. I suggest in this case we take 871 as our starting date.

FRANCE

Being in the continental land mass of Europe, how do we define the location of the society that is France? Natural frontiers and language differences are of some help. Parts of it front on to the Mediterranean, the Atlantic, and the Channel. To the south west past the Pyrenees the Spaniards speak a different language, as do the Italians to the south east. The Alps separate Switzerland from France, but about 20% in Switzerland speak French. Language and the Rhine river separate France from Germany, but Alsace and Lorraine, presently French, have both languages and have been fought over for a thousand years. The Dutch in the north east have a different language, but about a third of Belgians, also north east, speak French.

The corpse of the Roman society was barely cold when Clovis, king of a group of Franks - a Germanic people - settled in part of what is now France. Between 486 and 507 the Franks pushed the Visigoths back into Spain, took over Burgundy, and defeated the Alemanni. (Allemagne is French for Germany today). But the Frankish kingdom broke up when Clovis died. Charles Martel (the Hammer) in the 700s pulled the east and west kingdoms together as Austrasia and his grandson Charlemagne (the Great) in about 800 AD united it all again and more, as Austrasia. But it was as much or more Germany as France. France was only 2 regions of 5 or more. There's no France recognizable yet, and I think we need to have some semblance of the right territory to start with.

I suggest we begin with the treaty of Verdun in 843 between Charles the Bald who was the first king of Western France, and his brother, later called Louis the German. They agreed to have as their inheritances what later became France and Germany respectively. There wasn't much progress beyond that until the time of Hugh Capet. His kingdom was the Ile de France area and his capital was Paris, a central position in the future France. When the Capets came to power in 987 France was about the size of 2 French Departments today. But by the end of that dynasty France was the size of 59 modern French Departments (there are about 95 today). There was a common justice and coinage, and the Pope was at Avignon. France had a pre-eminent position in Europe. That was in 1328. I think we can recognize that as phases 1 and 2, the formative and ascendancy phases for France, 843 - 1328 = 485 years.

GERMANY
Now that we're getting the idea of how to do this, let's tackle our most difficult case so far - Germany.
First, the name, Germany, is no help to us; it comes from the Latin Germanus, of Roman times.

The territory lacks natural frontiers: on the east, next to Poland, on part of the west with France, and the Low Countries, and to the north with Denmark. As to language, Austria to the south is German speaking, as is most of Switzerland.

Our starting point, though, is not too difficult. We can begin with Louis the German, in 843, the other side of the treaty of Verdun. It's in the development of its later existence as a society that problems arise.

There's the problem of the continuous entity called the Holy Roman Empire. It was neither Holy, nor Roman, nor Empire, but existed as a phantasmagoria for close to a thousand years. This began with Otto 'the Great', a Saxon, who was chosen "German' king in 936. In 962 he was crowned by the Pope as Holy Roman Emperor. Frederick Barbarossa (1152 - 1190) called the 'empire' located in 'Germany' and 'Italy' by this name. To him it was a universal empire established directly by God and equal in rank with the Church. He was crowned emperor in 1155. This title went with Germany until 1254, then came a break and after that it gradually became more an honorary title with little power. It ended when Napoleon captured Vienna in 1805 and defeated the Austrians and Russians at Austerlitz in 1806. So we have two starting dates, the concept, in 936, with Otto; and the recognition, 962, when the Pope needed Otto's help. If we take the earlier date, 936, we have 936 - 1806, = 870 years. I would say it was never really a society, more a papal reward for good service. If we are to recognize it as a society, then it seems to me it has to be an Austrian rather than a German society. It distracted Germanic kings from their own territory into wars in northern Italy and dealings with the popes at Rome. But we have our date for the start of Germany - 843 AD.

RUSSIA

Russia is further removed from the Roman Empire than the other societies we've discussed, so we're not looking for a start that has to be after the death of the Rome society. Where did the word 'Russia" come from? The 'Russ' were asked by the local population to come to Novgorod to put an end to local in-fighting. As a result, the first 'Prince' of Novgorod was a 'Russ' in 862.

Who were these 'Russ'? In 945 there was a treaty with Byzantium. It had 3 Slav signatures and 50 Norse signatures. The Russ were Norsemen. And so we can say that Russia began in 862.

SECTION 2

CHAPTER 6
ROME AND VENICE
THE FORMATIVE AND ASCENDANCY PHASES

CHAPTER 7
ROME AND VENICE
EXPANSION: THE CANNIBALISTIC PHASE

CHAPTER 8
ROME AND VENICE
THE CANNIBALISTIC WAY TO DOMINANCE

CHAPTER 9
ROME AND VENICE
THE PHASE OF DOMINANCE

CHAPTER 10
ROME AND VENICE
DECLINE, DECAY AND DEATH

CHAPTER 6

ROME AND VENICE
THE FORMATIVE AND ASCENDANCY PHASES

Now that we know societies can live 1200 to 1400 years and we've traced the creation of some of our contemporary Nation Societies, before we analyze any of their rather complicated and incomplete lives further, let's compare and contrast two completed societies to get a fuller perspective on how the lives of our contemporary societies may continue to unfold. I suggest we choose Venice, an Island City Society as one, and Rome, a Land City Society, as the other. Venice lived and died earlier in our present Western Civilization, Rome lived and died in the dead Mediterranean Civilization, so this will be a good test for us as to whether there are life form similarities as well as obvious differences in life styles between dissimilar types of societies living in different civilizations.

Don't underestimate the power of Venice in its prime. The English playwright Shakespeare, in a different language in a different society, didn't compose one of his most successful plays called The Merchant of Genoa, or Florence, or Padua, or Pisa, or even Rome. He called it The Merchant of Venice.

THE FORMATIVE PHASE
Each society develops its own ethos, values, and way of succeeding in the world. It has its own peculiar problems to solve, and how it does or does not solve them helps set the course of its destiny. Island City Societies seem particularly suited to success in commercial activity, perhaps because lacking natural resources they have to live by their wits. They become great trading societies. Venice quickly developed a

monopoly in salt, and soon afterwards in high quality glass making, using the fine sand from its shores. The Venetians had a problem with water. They had too much of it. The sanitation difficulties were never satisfactorily solved, but their habitat caused them to invent the gondola for transportation, and to become expert sailors and later seamen with fast cargo-carrying galleys.

Land based societies seem more militarily inclined. Rome, an extreme example, early on showed no proclivity to trade, but was continually engaged in warfare, from the very beginning of its existence. In 753 BCE a god (Romulus, actually a half-Immortal, son of the god Mars and a human king's daughter) was supposed to have harnessed a plough and ploughed a furrow around the Palatine hill where the city was to be. He lifted the plough where the gates were to be set (Latin: portare, to carry, so porta, a gate, and our words porter, and portal, now used on the Internet). From this simple example we can see the strength of the influence of Rome through its language, even to this day in our own times.

Apparently the earliest citizens included descendants from the refugees after the fall of Troy city. Rome was created by them and the Latins, one of six peoples then inhabiting the peninsula we now call Italy. It was a very small city to start with, on one of 7 barren hills with a mosquito infested swamp in the middle, next to a river. Rivers have always been important to societies, for drinking water from upstream and carrying away waste downstream. Rome gradually expanded to include the seven hills, solved its marsh and bridge problems and in the process developed engineering and construction ability leading it to mastery of techniques for making concrete, building roads, viaducts, arched bridges, water transportation systems, baths, central heating systems, large buildings, and so on. Its soldiers doubled as engineers.

At first Rome was governed by kings who ruled for life. By 493 BCE kingship was abolished. The city controlled the surrounding 240 square miles, and had set up good government with a senate, consuls, tribunes, and so on. The city walls were 13 feet thick and 50 feet high. During this first 270 years the city established itself and provided security from attacks.

Good government and freedom for the citizens is at its best in the early stages of a society. In the first formative period of Venice, the chief advisor to Theodoric the Great, king of the Ostrogoths (471 - 526 AD) wrote:

"There is no distinction between rich and poor; the same for all. The houses are all alike... all your activity is devoted to the salt works, whence comes your wealth..."

In the formative phase of Rome two Tribunes of the people (the plebs, or lower order) were set up. They were plebians, elected for one year. Their duty was to protect the people against the magistrates. If any one, even a consul, wished to arrest a plebian, the Tribune could simply place himself before the threatened man and no one dared oppose his defence. Whoever did resist a tribune of the people was sacrificed to the gods, - put to death and his goods confiscated. A Tribune could not leave Rome and had to keep his house open day and night so no one would be unable to come to him. The Tribunes could stop any legislation they thought unwise by simply saying "veto" (I forbid). Unfortunately these early freedoms soon vanished in both societies.

. . . .

THE ASCENDANCY PHASE

We left Rome at about 493 BCE at the end of its formative phase. Its next stage is what I call the ascendancy phase. By the end of this phase in 266 BCE Rome had conquered all the other peoples in "Italy". Rome was now relatively secure with the Alps to the north and water surrounding the peninsula of "Italy". The Romans were very thorough. In one instance the Romans had besieged a city for 10 years, paid the Roman soldiers wages (a first in those days), took the city, massacred or sold the population, divided up the territory and desolated the city. That's how determined they were in conquering the whole of the peninsula. Their military organization was very orderly and innovative, but they had trouble with the Gauls in the north. They were beaten several times by the Gauls, but finally defeated them. The Roman army discipline was severe, even by the standards of its time. If a legion failed in its objective it was 'decimated'. One man in ten was put to death.

As the Romans conquered other territories they sent permanent garrisons of soldier farmers there to colonize the areas and secure their authority. They sent 20,000 farmers to Venusia to settle there and keep watch on the Venusians. Their famous Roman roads were necessary to move armies quickly and in relative safety. The roads were wide, straight, with a good foundation and pavement and cleared for a hundred yards on each side to reduce risk of ambush.

. . . .

The ascendancy phase of Venice was from 697 AD to 968 AD. Early in this period the 2nd Doge made trade agreements with the Longobards who had swept down on the Italian peninsula. But the Doge still professed loyalty to the Emperor of Byzantium (Leo III). Venice from now on was the principal outport in northern Italy of the Byzantine Empire. During 814 in a treaty between East and West a representative from Venice was present and its political existence was accepted.

Troubled by pirates in the Adriatic sea from the areas now Croatia and Herzegovina, Venice established defensive bases on their shores.

Byzantium called on Venice to sail as an ally against the "Saracens" (Arabs) threatening their colonies, in Sicily and ancient Greater Greece. Each time Venice won it was given more trading privileges. Then a commercial treaty gave Venice a role in the markets and commerce of the mainland. Venetian coinage was widely accepted. Venice began trading in silk from the east, wood, iron, and military equipment. Venice sent a fleet to put down piracy. This was in defence of Byzantium's interests as well as its own.

By 968 AD Venice, the maritime ally of Byzantium, was the acknowledged prime seagoing trading power in the Mediterranean. Venetian fleets traded in grain, wine, oil; had a virtual monopoly in salt, controlling the means of production and distribution, and shipping had to be by Venetian ships.
Although not a major land power, by subtle diplomacy Venice had gained recognition and respect and was present to protect its interests when treaties were negotiated.

The ascendancy phase of Venice lasted about 271 years.
. . . .

This has taken us from 421 AD, the year of the creation of Venice, to 697 AD as its formative phase (276 years), and from 697 to 968 AD, the end of its ascendancy phase (271 years).

Rome was created in 753 BCE, Its formative phase was to 493 BCE (260 years) and its ascendancy phase ended in 266 BCE (227 years).

The historical dates, in particular for the ascendancy phase of Venice, are not definitive. They're meant to identify in real terms the movement of a society from one stage in its life to the next, just as in individual lives there is no specific physiologically significant moment for the onset of puberty or menopause.

I have called the next phase expansion: the cannibalistic phase, because societies at this stage are now well grown with an established role in the civilization they find themselves in, but are not content to continue growing naturally. They are met with a competent rival society and generally fight it out until one is eliminated. As their population grows they send out colonies and establish trading centres in the territory of others. Militarily they develop an appetite for eating up weaker societies because now it's easier for them to seize the wealth of others than it is to go on creating it in their home territory.

So far we can see the smaller and more defensive society of Venice took longer to move through its first two phases of life than did Rome, a more powerful and aggressive society. Next we want to see how they live through their expansion, the cannibalistic phase each of them is about to enter.

CHAPTER 7

ROME AND VENICE
EXPANSION: THE CANNIBALISTIC PHASE

By 266 BCE Rome had secured for itself control over the Italian peninsula. It could have been satisfied with this success and developed trade and political relationships with the rest of the known world. During its conquest of Italy there had been several treaties of peace with Carthage, which had even at one time sent a fleet to help the Romans. Carthage controlled all of Sicily except for the Greek colony of Syracuse. The Greeks were allies of the Romans and when trouble erupted within their colony, Rome apparently became jealous of the prosperous Carthaginian and Greek colonies in Sicily, the next door island, and determined to take over. This involved declaring war on Carthage, in 264 BCE.

Rome was disciplined, efficient. Its citizens had a somewhat austere life style. Carthage was the greatest maritime trading power of its day and very wealthy. The first reaction to Rome's hostility was almost amused contempt. Rome would need a navy to get to Sicily. "Without our permission Rome cannot even wash her hands in the sea." Romans landed with help from a Greek fleet. A Greek general was king of Syracuse, the eastern part of Sicily. Rome attacked and scattered his army in 263 BCE, demanding 200 talents and promise of alliance. Then Rome attacked and destroyed two Carthaginian armies on the island. The city that had sheltered one asked for permission to surrender, but was refused. The Romans broke open the gates, pillaged the city and sold the inhabitants into slavery, (262 BCE). What followed was a 23 year war with Carthage, generally called the first Punic war; 'Punic' from Phoenicians, a famous seafaring people at the eastern end of the Mediterranean sea. Tyre, the mother city of Carthage had been one of their greatest cities. Carthage itself was on the north African shore line opposite Italy to the south of the Mediterranean.

Carthage naturally responded to Rome's attack by sending a fleet to ravage the coasts of Italy. The Romans had some smaller vessels but nothing to challenge the huge warships of Carthage. They decided to build warships and used as a model a Carthaginian ship wrecked on their coast. Their rowers practised on shore while the ships were being quickly built, with green wood. But when seaborne they fled on first contact with some ships from Carthage. Then the Romans designed a platform 36 ft by 4 ft attached to the mast of each ship with a huge spike on the end that was to be dropped. Now they sailed up to the ships from Carthage, dropped the platforms, the spikes drove into their decks and Carthaginian sailors were no match for the Roman soldiers who rushed on board. In 260 BCE the Romans took 30 ships from Carthage with this tactic.

A Carthaginian fleet was defeated in 256 BCE, but a subsequent siege of Carthage was unsuccessful.

Carthage did not fight its own battles. The generals and officers were from Carthage. The soldiers were hired foreigners. But the army was formidable. Each section kept its own language, protective dress and weapons: the African Libyans with pikes; Numidian horsemen wearing lion skins, with lances and bows, firing at full gallop; Iberians from Spain dressed in red and white, using swords; the Gauls, with shield and broadsword. Other races used bows and slings. The Carthaginians were no more merciful than the Romans. If their forces were defeated and survived, they were crucified.

In 250 BCE after a Roman victory over Carthage, 104 elephants were taken to Rome and slaughtered in the circus to amuse the people. Then two Roman fleets were destroyed in 249 BCE. But by 241 BCE Carthage was again defeated, made peace, and gave up Sicily.

At the end of the first Punic war Carthage agreed to pay Rome 3,200 talents within 10 years. With its resources spent the army went unpaid, causing a revolt. After 4 years most of these mercenaries had been put to death.

The payment to Rome (in 1999 US dollars) was about $100 million, coming from a world with just a fraction of our populations today. In 239 BCE Rome took advantage of the armed forces problems of Carthage to extract a further 1,200 talents (About $37.5 million US) plus Sardinia and Corsica.

The Gauls invaded Italy from the north and defeated one Roman army, but lost to two others. Rome established colonies among the conquered Gauls (218 BCE). In the same year Carthage attacked a rich city and took much booty. Rome claimed this contravened their treaty and demanded reparations. Carthage disagreed, and so began the second Punic war in 218 BCE.

Hannibal brought his Carthaginian troops from Spain across Europe into Italy. At Cannae Rome suffered the worst defeat in its history. 70,000 killed, only 3,370 escaping; 10,000 camp guards surrendered. Carthage lost 4,000 Gauls, 1,500 Spaniards and Africans. But Scipio finally defeated Hannibal at Carthage in 202 BCE. Rome's peace terms included surrender of all prisoners, elephants, and all but 10 warships, to enter no war without Rome's consent, plus payment of 250 talents a year for 50 years: (another $390 million US.) Carthage had ceased to be a great power.

In 197 BCE, a short 5 years later, Rome conquered Macedonia, its king had to surrender his fleet and all his possessions in Greece, and be an ally of Rome in future.

Rome next attacked the last remaining major power, Syria which lost 50,000 men in a rout costing Rome 300 - so Rome said. The Syrian king sued for peace, promised to surrender all his elephants and fleet, and pay 15,000 talents within 12 years. (Another $470 million US). Rome was now the undisputed most powerful state in its world.

Perseus became king of Macedonia, and amassed wealth, armies and allies in the near east. Rome declared war in 171 BCE. Perseus defeated a Roman army but sued for peace.
The reply was unconditional surrender. In 168 BCE he lost 20,000 killed and 11,000 prisoners. Rome claimed it lost 100.
The Roman soldiers became discontented because they had no chance to pillage the country. The Roman general ordered all the cities to collect their gold and silver. The Roman soldiers entered every city on the appointed day, sacked it, and 150,000 inhabitants were sold as slaves, the proceeds going to the soldiers. The Roman general brought back to Rome the spoils for a 3 day triumph. Day one: 250 chariots filled with statues and pictures. Day two: chariots loaded with arms; 750 vases filled with silver coins, each vase carried by 4 men; plus drinking vases, cups and flagons. Day three: young men carrying vases of gold and silver; 77 vases filled with gold pieces; a great golden vase studded with precious stones; plus 400 golden crowns from Greek cities. This is what I mean by a cannibalistic society.

Two years later in 149 BCE Rome began the third and last Punic war. Cato, a Roman senator had seen Carthage and was amazed at the wealth he saw there. He constantly argued for the destruction of Carthage. Meanwhile Carthage had been attacked by an African neighbour but Rome refused permission to retaliate, causing Carthage to have to agree to their demands. Then a Roman army of 80,000 landed in Africa near Carthage, which agreed to surrender. Rome promised

Carthage its liberty and laws, but ordered 300 hostages to go to Sicily, all arms to be given up. Carthage sent her ships, 200,000 stacks of arms and 3,000 engines of war. Next the Roman consuls said the Carthaginians must leave the city and go back 10 miles from the coast. This meant becoming peasants and losing their livelihood and source of wealth in trade and commerce.

Realizing it had been fooled, Carthage prepared for war as best it could, and drove back the first two Roman attacks. Then a new Roman general came, the adopted grandson of the Scipio who defeated Hannibal. In a complicated siege he starved the city into final surrender. When the city was torched the fire lasted 17 days. Then the city was demolished, the ground ploughed up and a priest put a curse on whoever should occupy the soil. The year was 146 BCE. The territory of Carthage was made a Roman province.

Next Rome overcame an uprising in Macedonia, also made a province. In the same year, 146 BCE Corinth, the richest city in Greece, rose against Rome. The city was sacked and destroyed and the inhabitants sold into slavery. All the works of art, some said to be the most beautiful in the world, were sent from Corinth to Rome.

But Rome was far from content with such conquests and looting. Spanish wars followed which went on for 70 years. Various Roman armies were defeated or massacred but eventually Rome prevailed. The Scipio who had destroyed Carthage was sent to Spain. He starved a city, whose inhabitants killed one another rather than surrender. He destroyed the city to the ground, leaving no trace to show where it had been (133 BCE). That finally subdued Spain.

I suggest this ends the first part of the expansion, the cannibalistic phase of Rome: 266 BCE to 133 BCE, 133 years.

In that period Rome wantonly defeated city after proud and wealthy city, stripped it, destroyed it, and sold its survivors into slavery for profit. Instead of expanding into other territories by commerce and colonies, it preferred the quicker more brutal method of sacking and looting territories. Rome combined the expansion phase, which I would expect to occur after the ascendancy phase, with the cannibalistic period. Its colonies were primarily military outposts keeping watch on its conquests. Rome developed a technique for exacting tribute, stripping its provinces of wealth and produce, while funneling these gains to Rome.

VENICE

We previously established the ascendancy phase as ending at about 968 AD. Here, with a trading society rather than a land based military society, the more normal development of expansion takes place next, with only such violence as necessary to maintain its position. I would include the incident of the fleet sent to crush the pirates at their home base, Lagosta, (1000 AD) as fitting this interpretation. Venice benefitted greatly financially from the first three Crusades (1096-9, 1147-9, and 1189-93), received additional territory, trading locations and privileges, and its role as sea power ally for Byzantium increased. A sizeable colony for a city of 150,000, the Venetians were said to number 200,000 in Constantinople by 1171. That was the year many of these Venetian merchants were arrested for arrogant brawling and terrorizing the other citizens, and their goods were confiscated. This so angered Venice that a hasty attack in reprisal followed which became a complete disaster. But by 1198 Venetian merchants were once more freed from customs duties as Byzantium needed the help of Venice against the Turks.

True to form for a trading society, Venice agreed to transport the 4th Crusade (1202) to the Holy Land for a rather exorbitant price, 85,000 marks, cash in advance, plus half of all conquests. To put this in perspective: in 1192 Richard 1st, king of England, who defeated Saladin during the 3rd Crusade, but was captured on his way home through Europe, was held to ransom for 150,000 marks. This was never paid in full and the resources of all England were taxed to the utmost for the first instalments.

But Venice turned into a cannibalistic society when part of its price, which the Crusaders didn't have, caused it to play the leading role in sacking Constantinople, capital of Byzantium, its former friend, ally and benefactor (see Chapter 3). Venice in this phase was aggressively expanding its territory and looting as well as trading. It fought many wars, including those against its rival Genoa: (1258, won; 1264, won; 1294 won once, lost once; 1299, crushing defeat; 1353 loss of entire fleet; 1381 lost the first battle, then trapped the Genoese fleet which surrendered. Genoa never recovered). Possession of eastern Mediterranean territories was involved in these wars that were fought through the period of the plague of the Black Death (1347-51) which killed a quarter to a third of the population of Europe.

During this period Venice was also fighting wars with Hungary for territorial possessions, including Dalmatia. That the rule of Venice was not benign is shown by Crete, acquired in 1212, but which revolted in 1364. I suggest the cannibalistic phase of expansion for Venice began in 1204 with the sacking of Constantinople, and continued through the Genoese wars to 1381.

Our tracking of Rome and Venice so far has given us (all numbers are years):

ROME (BCE). . . . .VENICE (AD)
753-493 (260). . . . .421-697 (276) FORMATIVE
493-266 (227). . . . .697-968 (271) ASCENDANCY

266-133 (133). . . . . EXPANSION with cannibalism
. . . . .968-1204 (236) without cannibalism
. . . . .1204-1381 (177) with cannibalism

We can see that Venice was not big enough or the type of society to begin its expansion phase with cannibalism, unlike Rome which had the power to do it. And Rome was such a huge society for its time that we'll have to conclude our discussion of the rest of its cannibalistic and expansionary phase next.

CHAPTER 8

ROME AND VENICE
THE CANNIBALISTIC WAY TO DOMINANCE

The second part of the expansion phase of Rome, with its cannibalistic period, begins, I suggest, at about 133 BCE. Rome became a different city, with a more cosmopolitan people. Rome had begun as a farm based community and the rigorous hard-working farm life persisted throughout its early development. Now a more luxurious life came with the spoils of war and there were slaves to do the work. Many slaves were brought to Rome. Immigrants poured in. Some of these newcomers were more literate than the Romans and often became tutors for the children of wealthy Roman citizens. Roman dress became more sophisticated with expensive oriental or Greek imports replacing the old woollen togas. Food, once coarse, was now more varied and of better quality. The Greek gods were recognized as the same beings worshipped as Roman gods. Eastern religions were tolerated. Early Romans had no books or theatre. After the conquest of Greece educated people spoke Greek and Greek philosophy and literature became known to the Romans. Greek works were translated into Latin.

The Romans had adopted the Etruscan custom of gladiatorial combats. For public entertainment wild beasts were brought from foreign lands and let loose in the circus, where trained hunters were employed to kill them. This was called a hunt. In 108 BCE 63 panthers were killed in a single hunt.

The farmer/soldiers/peasants were a disappearing breed. Some were killed in foreign wars or remained in conquered territory, still others couldn't get back from the campaigns to work their land each year. Those who did return could not sell their grain at a living wage because there was pillage instead of peasantry. Rome now imported tribute, including grain, from Sicily and Africa. The nobles bought the peasants land, formed large estates, and used slaves to do the work.

Roman women left behind no longer stayed at home and wove wool. They drove chariots, went to the circus, the theatre, public baths, and dined in public. Divorce became permissible and increasingly frequent. Before AD 1 marriage came to be regarded as a temporary union. 4 or 5 wives in succession were common. Pompey had 5, Caesar had 4.

Rome had so many slaves now that there was a revolt of about 200,000 of them in Sicily. It lasted 3 years. Finally put down in 132 BCE thousands of the slaves were crucified. There was another slave revolt in Sicily in 103 BCE and one in Italy, led by Spartacus and other gladiators, in 73 BCE. After defeating two small Roman armies this was crushed and the survivors, said to number about 6000, were crucified.

In addition to revolts there were civil wars. These went on for about 100 years.

In northwest Asia Minor the last king of Pergamon left his kingdom to the Roman people (132 BCE). This became the province of Asia.

Having made a territory into a subject province, the Romans generally furthered their own interests and not those of the province. Governors often imprisoned, whipped or executed subjects at will. They tended to rob temples of treasure and force cities and the wealthy to give them money, art and valuables. Governors only had one year in office so they had to make their fortunes quickly. A governor could station his troops where he wanted and cities paid him to keep them away. There were Roman laws against this type of extortion, but poorly enforced. A governor brought friends, officers and lawyers, and the whole retinue was generally on the make.

The unfortunate inhabitants of a province had to render a proportion of their harvest, a tribute in silver, and a tax for each family. It didn't end there. There were the publicans. They purchased from Rome the right to collect taxes, custom duties and rents. Each publican had his staff of clerks and collectors. The people were forced to pay more than was due and the word publican came to mean robber.

There was social unrest during this phase. Dispossessed peasant farmers, immigrants, freed slaves, flocked to Rome, without means for support. In the past when territory was conquered the State of Rome became the owner. Some land was left with the inhabitants who paid tribute for the use of it; ploughed lands and pastures were farmed out to companies of contractors (Publicans) who sublet and levied taxes. What was left after the various partitionings was regarded as waste land, available to any Roman citizen including retired soldiers, free, to take possession and settle. Some settlers had now been in possession for generations. Tiberius Gracchus carried out agrarian reform by leaving these occupants with about 320 acres each, taking the rest for distribution to poor citizens, a 30 acre lot in Italy for each family. There was a riot by the senators and other wealthy citizens. Tiberius and his supporters were clubbed to death. But not before Tiberius had monthly grain provided to the people of the city at half price. The agrarian 'reform' law was not repealed and the commissioners continued to distribute the land. About ten years later (123 BCE) his younger brother Gaius carried out more reforms - a corn law and free clothing for soldiers. Judges were no longer to be senators. Gaius and 3,000 of his supporters died in civil uprisings.

There was a 'social war' between Rome and its allies after a 95 BCE law forbidding allies to settle in Rome and claim to be citizens. The other Italians created their own capital and drove back the first Roman army. But with reports of uprisings in Spain, Gaul and Asia, a law was passed granting Roman citizenship to all Rome's allies who had not revolted on condition they adopted Roman law. Rome fought the other allies and won, executing the chief instigators and driving other leaders naked from the towns. One Samnite army held on. Then Rome extended the freedom of the city to all Italians (89 BCE). But this internal war probably cost about 300,000 lives. It's said the registry of citizens rose from 394,336 to about 900,000.

Meanwhile Mithridates, king of Pontus (an area south of the Black Sea opposite the Crimean peninsula) organized a larger kingdom around the Black sea. His father was a Persian king and his mother a Greek princess from Syria. The Greeks in the Roman province of Asia were being stripped of their wealth and resources. Mithridates, Rome's last great adversary in the east, took over, and abolished all taxes. The Greeks massacred the Italians there, said to be about 80,000, and took their valuables. Two Roman generals, Marius and Sulla, competed for the right to lead the forces going east to quell the uprising. 6 Roman legions entered Rome in support of Sulla, armed, the first time the rule against this was broken. Marius fled to Africa. Sulla led the forces to Greece and began conquests and massacres there. But in Rome supporters of Marius entered the city and massacred the leading senators. Sulla was declared a public enemy and V. Flaccus sent to Greece with another army. This mutinied. Flaccus was captured and killed. His second in command (Fimbria) led the army against Mithridates, but it deserted and joined Sulla, causing Fimbria to commit suicide. Sulla demanded 20,000 talents from Asia, which ruined it. His soldiers pillaged the province.

Having accomplished his mission with much brutality, Sulla returned to Rome with 40,000 devoted soldiers. 6 armies were raised against him. One killed its general for trying to force it to fight Sulla, who defeated another army. This was the first time two Roman armies fought each other (84 BCE).

The supporters of Marius left Rome after a massacre of more senators. Sulla fought the other armies, finally won, and had them all massacred, including those who surrendered. Then his soldiers began a general civilian massacre that went on for days.

Sulla settled 120,000 veterans on lands of those he had exterminated. He freed all slaves of the proscribed. 10,000 of them became his bodyguard. But 3 years after he became dictator Sulla abdicated, and soon after this he died.

Pompey was Sulla's favourite general. Pompey and Crassus arrived at Rome, each with an army for support. They met, and arranged that both would be elected consuls.The civil wars continued in Spain and Lusitania (Portugal). Then there was another slave revolt in Sicily. A tribune publicly denounced the governor of Sicily (Verres). His accuser before the tribunal was the youthful Cicero. Verres didn't deny the charges, merely said he used a third of the extortion money to buy his judges. He went into exile.

Pompey was given special powers to deal with the pirates who were now so bold and numerous as to have formed their own state, and were threatening Rome's supply routes. Pompey took command in 66 BCE. He cleared out the pirates in the central and eastern Mediterranean. Next he went to war with Mithridates who committed suicide to avoid capture. Pompey made Syria a province, then took Jerusalem. But back at home Italy was full of social unrest. When Caesar became dictator, with a population of about 2 million in Italy, there were 320,000 citizens being supported by the state. In 43 BCE Cicero, now a Roman statesman, spoke in the Senate of Rome:

"The budget should be balanced, public debt should be reduced, the arrogance of officialdom should be tempered and controlled and assistance to foreign lands should be curtailed lest Rome become bankrupt. The mob should be made to work and not depend on government for subsistence..."

Without detailing this further as we are merely noting a pattern, I suggest Rome is about to enter a new phase. This may have begun when Caesar defeated Pompey in 48 BCE, or when Caesar was murdered in 44 BCE, but about this time Rome began to settle down internally and externally to a new phase of unqualified dominance around the Mediterranean and beyond, despite some periods of poor leadership. And with this security Roman culture began to flourish.

VENICE

We left Venice in about 1381 AD after it had finally crushed Genoa as a rival sea power. We suggested Venice's cannibalism began with the sacking of Constantinople in 1204, but it could be said to have begun about 75 years earlier with Venetian attacks on Greek islands, including the stripping of Rhodes (see chapter 3). The later date was chosen because of the enormity of the attack on the capital of Byzantium and the consequent riches and territories with immediate elevation of Venice to world power.

During this cannibalistic phase Venice, as did Rome, experienced internal as well as external rebellion. We've already mentioned the rebellions in its overseas territories of Dalmatia and Crete, but in Venice itself in 1296 the Great Council was closed to the admission of new families and from then on Venice became an oligarchy. This caused a revolt in 1300 by the people excluded from a seat in the Great Council.

The uprising was quickly crushed. The doors were open to let the mob in: the ringleaders were promptly seized and hanged. But in 1310 there was another larger revolt. It too was crushed, one leader was killed, the other fled from Venice. This experience caused the establishment of the Council of 10. It began as a public safety committee to hunt down the conspirators. In 1335 it was made permanent.

The reaction of Venice to these events was to turn itself into a police state. Dissidents just disappeared. Spies and informers were everywhere and torture of prisoners was a common practice. This made a popular revolt impossible through personal fear of the consequences. A French ambassador to Maximilian called the Venetians 'crafty and malignant foxes' but also 'proud and ferocious lions' and 'whales who besiege the ocean.'

. . . .

Rome achieved some stability by about 44 BCE because the various military aspirants for power fought it out with their respective armies until one was victorious. Venice achieved stability by about 1381 AD through financial freedom and wealth satisfying the merchant class and political power held by an oligarchy operating a police state.

This concludes our view of the Formative, Ascendancy and Expansion phases of our two examples, Rome and Venice. We can now complete the Expansion phase for each:

EXPANSION
ROME (BCE). . . . .VENICE (AD)
. . . . .968 - 1204 (236) without cannibalism
266 - 44 (222). . . .1204 - 1381 (177) with cannibalism

In the life of societies the phase of dominance comes next and we'll see how Rome and Venice experience this period in their lives and how long it lasts for each of them.

CHAPTER 9

ROME AND VENICE
THE PHASE OF DOMINANCE

ROME

Dominance for Rome lasted from the 40s BCE to about 180 AD. The beginnings of this phase continued the brutal civil wars with Roman armies fighting one another. This ended when Cleopatra (for whom Caesar had fathered a child and gave her Egypt to rule), and Anthony, committed suicide. There was a triumvirate or three headed rulership to solve the civil wars problem, but this soon became a single dictatorship. Caesar said he had killed a million men and sold another million into slavery. This type of military conduct had certainly crushed resistance in the provinces. They became Romanized with road systems, public buildings, senates, assemblies, and judicial systems of their own. With peace at last the provinces grew and prospered and provided the finest part of Roman armies. Trajan was the first Roman Emperor born and raised in a Roman colony - Spain.In the early days of this phase, when heredity still decided who ruled, Claudius is an interesting example. It's been said that Claudius was found by the Praetorian guard in the palace hiding in a closet after the murder of Caligula, and the Praetorians had him proclaimed Emperor. He didn't run the government. He had 4 freedmen to do that. As they were former slaves this upset the nobles in the Senate who had to co-operate with them.

Claudius is generally regarded as simple minded, with nodding head, stammering, and trembling hands, foolish jokes and laughable edicts to the people on wine making or eclipses rather than affairs of state. But how does one explain his relationships with women. He repudiated his first two wives for evil conduct and then married Messalina. We're told she had a competition with her chief maid; Messalina having intercourse with 23 men in one night while the maid only managed 19.

Claudius had Messalina put to death. But he was apparently responsible for a naval battle between two fleets on a lake involving 19,000 condemned men from across the empire. Engines of war were put around the lake to make the men fight. And in the reign of Claudius the Jews were expelled from Rome. Yet in certain ways he tried to be a benevolent leader and some of the harsher laws were softened under his rule.

Many of the ancient families of Senators had been massacred in civil wars. Short of funds through intemperate extravagance, such as Caligula with his million dollar suppers, Nero travelling with an entourage of 1000 chariots or his wife Poppae taking along 500 asses for her daily milk baths, the hereditary rulers condemned a number of the surviving senators for treason. This was usually done so that their wealth could be confiscated for the imperial treasury. Some wealthy citizens even went so far as to commit suicide before being accused to be more sure their children could inherit their estates.

When the degenerate hereditary rulers had been cleared away, either by suicide (Nero) or assassination, (Caligula, Claudius), rulers chosen by various army groups came to be emperors, 3 in one year (68-9 AD) Galba was murdered, Otho chose suicide, Vitellius was murdered. From then on rulers were chosen by merit, beginning with Vespasian, (69 - 79). His grandfather was a centurion. Sculpture shows this general to have been square faced and thin lipped. He restored order and discipline, was very economical, lived simply, and worked to the day of his death. He created new senators from the great Provincial families that had come into being in Spain and Gaul. The various provincial revolts were put down and Rome's true dominance took shape.

During this phase of the society Pax Romana came into effect - the universal Roman peace. Industry, trade and commerce in the empire could thrive. There was trading even as far as to India and China. In our century the sunken remains of two Roman ships each laden with jars, presumably with contents for trading, were found in the Amazon basin, in South America. The city of Rome, now with a population close to two million was a centre for luxury goods, but began to develop a negative balance of trade as its appetite for luxury exceeded its exports.

We should not underestimate Roman society achievements, many created during the dominance phase. There was rotation of crops and soil fertilization. Rome had the first state hospital in the western world, the first free health service for the poor, the first distribution of food, wines, clothing and even money to poor people on designated lists. There were urban cohorts who patrolled the streets at night to minimize crime and they doubled as firefighters. There was an elaborate government postal service. A map of all the roads in the Empire was carved in stone and set up in a public place. Copies were made for use by travellers. In Rome there were covered malls for citizens to walk about protected from the weather.

Rome's public spectacular events in the Circuses were free. They generally ran from morning to evening and included four horse chariot racing. There were professional drivers and chariot companies competing much as our car racing of formula 1 cars is organized today. Several circuses existed in Rome. The largest, the Circus Maximus, had accommodation for 250,000 spectators. The Coliseum seated 87,000 with standing room for 15,000.

Let's just take one example of how the society operated - its use of water. A clean abundant water supply is essential to good human health. The water supply to Rome was 300 million gallons a day. It was carried in by 10 aqueducts. There were nearly 260 miles of conduits, 20 supported by arches and columns. The Romans knew how to prevent hammering in the supply lines by setting up large columns filled with air leading off the supply, just as in a good modern plumbing system a 6 inch dead end air-filled pipe line is attached close to each tap or valve to let the air cushion any sudden stoppage of water rushing at 125 lbs per square inch. If this buffering is not set up the pipes "hammer" noisily when a tap is quickly shut off. The Roman water supply is said to have been better than in 19th c. AD London or Paris.

Some of the water supply was for the public baths. These had large marble tanks of cold water with storage and furnace rooms. There were sweating rooms, heated halls with small bathrooms leading off them. There were huge covered malls, dressing rooms, rubbing rooms, all paved with mosaics and with pictures hung and statues. Outside were gardens enclosed by a portico, library, gymnasium and changing rooms.

Country houses had parks, land under cultivation, reservoirs for fish breeding, aviaries for rare birds, underground galleries for use in hot weather and a centrally heated floor system for cold weather. There were kitchens, laundries, a mill, oven, spinning and weaving rooms and slave cabins, in some cases a slave village with hundreds of slaves.

The Roman army was another remarkable achievement of the Roman society. Many generals in subsequent periods have studied Roman logistical skills, strategy and tactics in the field of battle. There were 25, later 30 legions with 6000 men in each, These were volunteers, usually poor people who enlisted for 20 years and often for a second term. They were paid wages. At the end they received a lump sum of money and gift of land. In addition to the legions there were auxiliaries - cohorts of infantry and squadrons of cavalry. A soldier could not be promoted beyond centurion, in charge of 100 men. Our equivalent would be a non-commissioned officer such as an army company sergeant major. The legion was divided into cohorts and battalions. Only a senator could be a legate and command a legion. A knight or equestrian could be a procurator or commander of a cohort.

In 9 AD the Germanic people beyond Gaul surprised a Roman army in ambush and massacred it. Verus, the commanding officer committed suicide as did some of his senior officers, the remaining officers were buried alive or crucified. The legions destroyed were 17, 18 and 19. They were never re-instituted. Unlike past periods in Roman history the Emperors decided against subjugating the Germanic people.

Much later in this phase of dominance the emperor Trajan (98-117 AD) decided to attack the Dacian people, took their capital, and the Dacian king committed suicide. Trajan made it the province of Dacia, Romanized it with colonies, operated mines, cultivated the land and built cities. Latin became the chief language. This area later became Romania.

Trajan then turned his attention to the Parthians who frequently gave trouble in the furthest east of the Empire. He had boats dismantled and carried overland in wagons to the Euphrates river, entered Babylon, then overland again with the boats to the river Tigris where he took two major Parthian cities. He died on the march, but had made three new provinces: Armenia, Mesopotamia and Assyria.

I suggest this was the last offensive action of the empire, which had now reached its greatest extent in 117 AD in the late middle of the phase of dominance. Although as you know by now I'm not really interested in individual performances they certainly lend more colour to the narrative of the advance, pre-eminence and decline of societies. So let's look at the power of Roman society in this phase of dominance as if it were through the eyes of Hadrian, who was selected by Trajan as his successor.

Hadrian (117 - 138) swore never to put a senator to death, attended conscientiously to business, heard complaints in person, said

"I wish to govern the republic not as my property but as that of the people."

He lived like a private citizen, without luxury, eating simple meals. He was fluent in Greek, learned painting and sculpture, geometry, music, medicine.

His first act was to abandon Trajan's eastern conquests around the Euphrates. He thought the empire was large enough already. He avoided war, kept peace with surrounding tribes by making presents to their chiefs. During his reign the frontiers were never attacked. But he ensured good armies and discipline, did away with officers' banquet halls, drove out the actors and jugglers, ordered at least three marches a month, laid down rules for camps and baggage and had lighter engines of war. In camp he lived like a common soldier, led military marches of 18-19 miles on foot, fully armoured. He visited sick soldiers, gave promotions for bravery or long service. His men were devoted to him. There were no mutinies in his reign.

Hadrian spent his time travelling about his empire and organizing the government. He visited Syria, the Danube provinces, south and north Italy, Gaul, and Britain. Hadrian's wall exists there to this day, built to keep the Scots out. This wall was over 60 miles long from Solway Firth to the Tyne. It cut Scotland off from England. There was a ditch in front 40 feet wide and 15 feet deep. Behind it was a masonry wall 7 feet thick and 15 feet high guarded in front by 300 towers jutting out, backed by 80 guard posts. Along the full length of the wall ran a military road, 65 feet wide defended by 17 forts each within reach of water. A second ditch between 2 lines of earthworks protected the wall on the south. This was constructed by 3 legions.

Having dealt with the defence of Britain he moved on to Spain, all the African provinces, Syria, met the king of the Parthians, returned his daughter but not his golden throne, both taken by Trajan. Then he went to the provinces bordering the Black Sea. To Thrace, Adrianople (it's really Hadrianople), on to Macedonia, Epirus, Thessaly and Greece, returned to Rome by sea, stopping en route at Sicily.

He made a second voyage east, to Greece, Syria, Judaea, the Dead Sea and strongholds in the new province of Arabia. At Alexandria in Egypt he visited the famous library, then travelled up the Nile. In this way, following Hadrian, we can grasp the size of the Roman Empire in its phase of dominance and what was required to maintain it.

Hadrian's successor was Antonius(138-161 AD), selected by Hadrian. Antonius was a rich senator from Nimes in Gaul. He was economical and lived plainly. He refused the money usually offered to emperors, paid the soldiers' lump sum payments out of his own personal fortune. He built up a vast treasury of many hundreds of millions of dollars (in today's equivalent). There were no wars during his entire reign. "Better to save one citizen than kill 1000 enemies." We can see how far Rome had come from the boasts of Caesar about killing and enslaving men. All these leaders were the products of the age of their society.

Antonius had selected and adopted Marcus Aurelius to be his successor. Marcus Aurelius (161-180 AD) studied philosophy, became a Stoic, lived in perpetual austerity, worked hard, suffered poor health, perhaps induced when he slept on the ground in his youth. He detested war but had to devote years to defending the empire against peripheral enemies. The Parthians attacked Syria, the Moors attacked the Spanish coasts. The Germanic peoples in the Danube region attacked Greece, and even Italy, ravaging, plundering and taking the inhabitants. To make matters worse, Rome suffered a plague which reduced the army strength. Then there were poor harvests. Taxes were not coming in as usual and to defray costs, rather than trying to extract more from the people, Marcus Aurelius sold the palace jewels. He died, worn out, at what is now Vienna, preparing a second campaign in the Danube area.

As you can see, the peak of Roman dominance has now already passed. The greatest extent of the empire has come and gone, and the last twenty years of this phase see Rome beginning defensive wars against outside invaders. These are wars by a reluctant Rome which is merely trying to protect its existing territory.

. . . .

During this phase of dominance Roman government began with three branches of administration: accounts, despatches, and petitions, a fourth was soon added, investigations. The governors of the provinces were now salaried officials, left in charge for longer periods, as were the tax and other officials.

The Provinces kept their own revenues, paid all their own expenses and wealthy local citizens were encouraged to support their towns. Pliny the Younger gave over 11 million sesterces to his town for a library, school, temples, and covered malls for merchants during fairs (In 1999 $US about $13,750,000). Only Egypt remained under direct control of the emperors, because of the vital grain supply. No senators were allowed there, the administration was part of the personal estate of the emperor.

. . . .

Rome's greatest gift to later societies was probably its law. The jury decided questions of fact. Judges decided questions of law and could take previous opinions into account. The law had three branches:

jus (or ius) civile - civil law - for Rome and its citizens that in the dominance phase now numbered about 7 million. This law included statutes, decrees, edicts and ancient customs which were carefully preserved.

Jus gentium - the law for all others (gens = race, hence our word genocide) it included laws on slavery, private ownership of property, contract and partnership law.

Jus naturale - was the natural law of philosophers, the kind of law that in our modern era Rousseau and Tom Paine wrote about: the state of nature, all men as equal, with no exploitation.

To this day such concepts as 'habeas corpus" are still used in the Roman (Latin) language and define fundamental principles of our justice system.

. . . .

Public finance was another well organized system within the government. There were several branches:
1. the original senate treasury

2. the imperial treasury, the emperor's treasury or 'fisc' from revenue derived from the provinces, imperial domains - such as Egypt - taxes and customs duties.

3. the private fortune of the emperor

4. the military treasury, added during the early part of the phase of dominance. To fund this treasury there was a 1% sales tax, a 5% tax on the emancipation of slaves, and a 5% tax on larger inheritances.

. . . .

Judaea

Since we have regarded Hadrian as representing the spirit of his age we can discuss how he made, I believe, one unfortunate mistake. The Romans had been sensitive to the religion of the Jews. For example, because it forbade graven images the Romans issued coins for Judaea which did not have the head of the Emperor embossed on them. Further, the Jews were exempt from military service. They were allowed to keep their Council of Ancients (Sanhedrim). Roman soldiers were forbidden to carry their standards into the city of Jerusalem. Romans were forbidden to enter the Temple. The wealthier Jews were friendly towards Roman rule, bringing peace and stability, but a party known as the Zealots in particular thought it sacrilege to obey a foreign unbeliever and pay him taxes. In 66 AD the revolt became general. The Zealots drove the rich citizens from Jerusalem, seized the Temple and king's palace, and finally massacred the Roman soldiers and leaders of the Roman party. The governor of Syria came with an army but was defeated. Nero sent Vespasian with an army of about 50,000. He began a deliberate campaign, but returned with his army to Rome when proclaimed emperor (69 AD). He sent his son Titus with 60,000 men (70 AD). Titus besieged Jerusalem for months. There was famine. The walls were finally breached. The city was taken house by house, the palace stormed, then the Temple. All the inhabitants were massacred or sold into slavery. He took the sacred objects from the Temple with 700 prisoners for his triumph in Rome and left the city in ruins.

Now we come to Hadrian. The Zealots were rebelling again. Hadrian ordered a colony of veterans to be established on the site of the ruined city of Jerusalem. This provoked general rebellion. It took the governor of Syria 3 years to put it down. He took the strongholds one by one, said to be 50 fortresses and 985 towns (132-135 AD). In the campaign about 580,000 Jews were said to have perished. Hadrian renamed the province Palestinian Syria and put 2 legions there. The country was left a virtual desert. The Jews were forbidden under penalty of death to come within the limits of Jerusalem except once a year to weep at the foot of the city wall. The repercussions of these events have, I suggest, echoed down through the ages to the present day.

. . . .

Christianity
This came into existence during the phase of dominance in the Roman society. The Romans were tolerant of all religions including Christianity, but this particular religion presented them with some problems. First, the sect held secret meetings. This left Christians open to accusations of infanticide at such meetings, plotting against the state, and so on. Next, all the courts of law and appointments to office required swearing an oath by the gods. If they regarded the ancient Roman gods as impotent relics of the past it seems to me they should have had no problem obeying Roman law ("render unto Caesar the things which are Caesar's..." Matthew.22.21) because the 'gods' they were swearing to were meaningless to them. But many Christians did not see it that way. They refused to swear such oaths. This put them in direct conflict with Roman government and in breach of law and custom. It's true that Nero had some Christians put to death after the disastrous fire (64 AD) in Rome which began in an oil storage area and over many days swept through a large part of the city, which had to be rebuilt. Nero was apparently out of town when it began but a scapegoat had to be found as some were accusing Nero. Systematic persecution of the Christians did not come until after the phase of dominance.

. . . .

The arts
During this phase of dominance we have, as we would expect, almost the entire collection of writers, historians, philosophers, men of religion and medicine who lived in the Roman society:
from Italy; Cicero, Horace, Juvenal, Livy, Ovid, Pliny the Younger, Suetonius, Tacitus, Virgil,
from Greece; Epictetus, Galen, Lucian, Ptolemy,
from Spain; Lucan, Martial, Quintilian, Seneca,
from Judaea came the gospels of the New Testament of the Christian Bible; Matthew, Mark, Luke and John,
finally there came the famous Jewish historian, Josephus, Christian writer Tertullian, and convert to Christianity, Paul.

. . . .

During this phase of dominance, not content with chariot races and theatre with some gladiatorial combat as the main public spectacles, cruelty and bloodshed increased in shows at circuses. As early as 106 AD about 11000 wild animals were killed in circus events in one year. Later, naked prisoners of both sexes were tied to posts and predatory wild animals released to tear them apart and eat them. Some gladiatorial combats came to be more like small wars to the death. The frequency of crimes of violence increased in the city. The number of prostitutes in Rome increased to 32,000 or more. Homosexuality became common and even fashionable. We don't presume to pass moral judgements on these life styles, all we need to do is to notice that when they are prevalent or popular the society is entering the phase of decline and decay. Rome was now starting its slow decline towards its end.

. . . .

VENICE
The phase of dominance for Venice was roughly the same length of time as for Rome. I suggest this was from 1381 AD to 1574 AD, these being the usual markers for convenience and not meant to be exact dates for transitions. Just as Rome lost 3 legions to the Germanic people, so did Venice suffer defeat by the League of Cambrai. But as we saw (Chapter 4) Venice soon got most of its lost territory back, the chief effect

was in suffering financial cost. The quotation we gave from the Doge's speech (Chapter 3) sums up the dominance role of Venice. During this phase of dominance for Venice, as for Rome, the arts flourished (Chapter 4). As late as 1571 came success in the battle of Lepanto. In 1574 Venice could still build a complete galley in a few hours, but as with Rome the seeds of decline and decay were already present. Venice received little or no help in defending its own and eastern Mediterranean interests against the Turks. But it provided central Europe with some protection from what would otherwise have been a full onslaught by the expanding Turkish nation.

It is natural for a society at a certain phase in its development to expand, just as a tree has to grow somewhere and the forces of nature are so strong that a blade of grass can push its way up through asphalt. Problems arise because other entities already occupy the space where the expanding society needs to grow, and that causes competition, conflict, and the supremacy of the fittest.

This ends our discussion of the dominance phase of our two chosen societies. I suggest for Rome it was from about 44 BCE to 180 AD (224 years) and for Venice from about 1381 AD to 1574 AD (193 years).

CHAPTER 10

ROME AND VENICE
DECLINE, DECAY AND DEATH

The Rome society was a huge entity in its civilization. Its final phase took nearly 300 years. To attempt to present this fairly in just a few pages is quite a challenge. For easier reading it's been divided into separate sections in this order:

The Political Aspect
The Army
Finance, Economic Health, and Taxation
Beliefs

The Political section is the longest and contains some detail about an almost unending stream of civil wars, assassinations, murders, and rebellions. You may wish to skim through this and perhaps find the other sections of greater interest.

THE POLITICAL ASPECT
We left Rome at the death of Marcus Aurelius who was trying to keep the peripheral Germanic peoples from invading the Empire south of the Danube river. That was in 180 AD. Head of state succession always seemed to be a problem in the Roman society. The system of 'adopting' a 'son' who was not related but was very capable and then nominating him as a successor had worked well during the phase of dominance.
But unfortunately Marcus Aurelius had a real son, Commodus. He seemed satisfactory at first as a young man under the guidance of his father's friends but soon became the worst tyrant since Nero (who had Christians covered with bitumen and used as human torches for an evening garden party at the palace). Commodus called himself Hercules and posed with a lion's skin and club. He had all his father's friends and many of the Senators executed, paid no attention to his duties, and squandered the treasury. Grain distribution was halted. He

gathered the infirm and crippled, disguised them as monsters with serpents for tails, armed them with sponges that looked like stones and then killed them for sport with arrows. After 12 years of misrule a mob demanded his death. He was strangled by order of his wife and his officers.

The Senate replaced him with Pertinax, an old soldier, son of a freedman of ability who began as a charcoal burner, acquired wealth and a proconsulate. Pertinax stopped persecutions for treason, and recalled exiles. But after 87 days 300 praetorian guards marched on the palace and killed him (AD 193).

It was a custom for emperors to make donatives (donations) to soldiers on special occasions, such as being appointed Emperor, marrying, birth of a child, a victory in war. This was now abused -- the praetorians had 2 candidates bidding up the price of the donatives to become Emperor. The praetorians chose the higher bidder. But this didn't satisfy the 3 great armies of Syria, Britain and the Danube. Each proclaimed its own choice of Emperor. Severus of the Danube had the largest army (10 legions), was closest to Rome, and first to arrive there with an army. The praetorians didn't dare oppose him. The successful praetorian candidate-emperor was killed by order of the Senate. Severus as Emperor (194 AD) was a hard worker, left the senate little power, increased the pay of the soldiers, allowed their wives into camp. He defeated and killed the other two army candidates. Severus led an expedition against the Parthians in the east, took their capital and conquered Mesopotamia. Then he went with his two sons to Britain for a war with the Scots. He died there (211 AD).

The sons of Severus were made joint emperors, but Caracella, one of his sons, killed his brother, many more Senators, and his brother's friends. He issued an edict making all inhabitants of the Empire Roman citizens. This was no privilege. They now paid taxes as Roman citizens, and, it's said, as foreigners. Caracella was uncouth and lived like a common soldier. After a war against the Germanic people he went to Asia, stopping in Alexandria, a sophisticated city that laughed at him. He invited the leaders to eat with him, then had their throats cut and turned his soldiers loose to pillage the city and massacre at will. He attacked the Parthians and led his army beyond the Tigris. His praetorian prefect killed him (217 AD).

The Prefect led the army back to Syria and proclaimed himself Emperor. Caracella's mother came from a wealthy Syrian family. They promised much gold to the soldiers and a 16 year old boy candidate. The prefect was killed (218 AD).

The boy was obliged to adopt his cousin Alexander as his successor. Then he tried to kill Alexander. Soldiers stopped him and told him to end his riotous behaviour. Finally they killed him, and proclaimed his cousin emperor (222 AD). But Alexander could not control the soldiers. There was civil unrest in Rome, the Parthians were attacking in the east, the Germanic peoples in the west. (235 AD). This was a period of military anarchy. Various armies were each trying to make their general the emperor. The emperors spent their time and energy opposing their rivals. Each successful candidate was either assassinated or executed. Maximium, a huge man, once a Thracian shepherd, now a general, marched on Italy with the army of the Danube. They left a trail of pillage and massacre, all within the Roman Empire. He was killed by his soldiers. The Senate elected two others, the praetorians added a child, Gorelian, as emperor. The praetorians killed both the choices of the Senate. The child's stepfather governed for him (238-244AD) The Syrian army fighting the Parthians proclaimed as emperor an Arab, formerly a brigand chief, Philip. The Danube army revolted and proclaimed Dacius, then marched on Italy. Philip was defeated and killed. Dacius was killed 2 years later in a battle on the frontier in Thrace (251AD)

The son of Dacius, a child, was made joint emperor with Gallus, a general. Gallus had the child killed, but was killed by his soldiers. Valerian an elderly senator, governed from 251 - 264 AD but was captured by the Parthians. He died in captivity. It's said Sapor, the Parthian king, always used him as a foot rest to mount his horse.

New emperors were proclaimed by all the armies. Counting their sons, there were 30 in all, this was later called the period of the 30 tyrants. As soon as the frontier armies left their posts and began fighting among themselves, the frontier peoples began to invade the empire, now from 3 sides. The Parthians under King Sapor took Mesopotamia, and pillaged the proud and wealthy city of Antioch. The Franks ravaged their way through Gaul as far as Spain. The Alemanni even invaded Italy from the north. A new Germanic people appeared, the Goths. They settled on the coast of the Black Sea, near the mouth of the Danube. Then they crossed into Moesia and Thrace which they ravaged. The Empire lost all its possessions north of the Danube. The Goths fitted out ships with crews of Roman prisoners, then ravaged Greece.

Various Illyrian Emperors came and went. Then came Diocletian, in 284 AD, the son of a slave mother. Diocletian was helped by his colleague Maximian, who he made co-emperor (286). Between them they restored order. The peasants of Gaul had rebelled against the tax collectors and formed an army. Maximian exterminated them and repelled the Alemanii. Diocletian conquered the Parthians and took back Mesopotamia. Diocletian established himself in the east. Maximian went not to Rome but to Milan in the west for his seat of government. Diocletian reduced the size of the provinces; 57 now became 96. The governors no longer had armies to command. He and Maximian were called Emperors, 'Augustus'. Diocletian arranged for each to have an assistant called Caesar, to be an eventual successor. The four ruled the

Empire. They were all Illyrians, not Romans. After 20 years Diocletian abdicated in favour of his choice of Caesar and made Maximian do the same. The new emperors, each now Augustus, appointed their own successors as Caesars. But this system only worked while Diocletian was in effect the prime Emperor.

When one of the Emperors (Galerius) ordered a new property valuation the Romans rebelled and killed the prefect of the city. Maximian came out of retirement to become Emperor in 306 AD. Now came a war between the Emperors. There were 5 civil wars in 16 years. Severus entered Italy, was abandoned by his army and killed. There were now 7 emperors reigning at the same time:

Galerius and his appointment Lucinius (Illyrian, son of a peasant), Constantine, Maximinus, Alexander, Maxentius and Maximian (307AD). Maximian was forced to abdicate (again) and soon died. Maxentius defeated Alexander, later was defeated by Constantine and drowned. Galerius died. Maximinus was defeated by Lucinius and killed himself. His family was massacred. Then Constantine defeated Lucinius (314) and took his European Provinces. Lucinius was defeated again in 323, surrendered and was put to death in 324.

Constantine was now the only Emperor left. He is said to have been the eldest son of Constantius by a barmaid, and born at Nis in what is now Serbia. He established Constantinople in the east as his new capital. He was the only ruler for 13 years. He had his son Crispus and his friends put to death for an alleged conspiracy against him. He also executed the son of his sister. Constantine, like Diocletian, ruled not from Rome but in the east as an oriental despot. Ministries of state ran the empire. Each minister had a separate branch of the imperial services and carried out the emperor's orders.

In 337 Constantine's 3 sons succeeded him as joint emperors. The soldiers massacred the rest of his family. Constantine II was killed after defeating his brother Constans. Constans was killed by Magnentius. Constantius defeated Magnentius and was now sole emperor.

In 360 Julian was proclaimed emperor in Paris, in Gaul. He had defeated the Alemanni before becoming emperor. He died of injuries after defeating the Parthians. He was emperor for less than 2 years but was a brilliant man, said to be able to listen, converse and dictate with 3 different people at the same time on 3 different subjects without error. He was the last Emperor capable of running the Empire single-handed.

Valentinian, his successor, divided the empire with his brother Valens. He pushed the Germanic people back out of the imperial provinces. But the Goths who themselves had been pushed westwards had taken refuge within the empire and began a war against Valens, who was defeated and killed at Adrianople (378). The Goths invaded the empire. This was the beginning of the end for Rome.

Theodosius, now emperor, subdued the Gauls in the west. Gratian was assassinated and Maximian proclaimed Emperor (383). Theodosius defeated and killed Maximian. In 392 Arbogastes killed Valentinian II and proclaimed Eugenius emperor. In 395 Theodosius divided the empire between his two sons Honorius and Arcadius. He died in 402, 8 years before the sack of Rome..

Alaric, King of the Goths, invaded Italy. The Vandals, Suevi and Burgundians invaded Gaul. In 404 came the last Roman triumph. Stilicho, a Germanic and a general, with Honorius the weak young emperor, rode through Rome to celebrate the general's victory in driving Alaric from Greece. In 406 Stilicho defeated the Germanics pouring Into Italy from the north. Most of the Roman army was now Germanic. In 407 Stilicho recalled the last of the Roman Legions from Britain for war against the Goths. As a result, the Scots broke into Caledonia. The Romans in Britain wrote "To Actius the consul at Rome: the groans of the British. The barbarians drive us to the sea, the sea drives us back to the barbarians, between them we are either slain or drowned." In 408 the irresponsible young emperor Honorius had Stilicho killed. He was foolishly afraid of Stilicho's ability and power. In the same year Alaric invaded Italy.

Alaric, King of the Goths, stood with his hostile army of Goths before the gates of Rome in 410 AD. This had not happened to Rome in the 600 years since Hannibal faced Rome with his Carthaginian army. Then, Rome was in its ascendancy phase. There were three armies drawn up between Hannibal and the city. The fortifications were in good order. Every able bodied man in Rome had received military training. The citizens were proud of their city and would fight without question to protect it. Other armies could be raised and might soon appear. Hannibal was a military genius, but he decided not to attack Rome. He was far from home, rapid reinforcements would be hard to come by for him but not for the Romans. Instead he roamed through Italy for 16 years. The Romans harassed his forces but never risked a pitched battle. Then he left, and Rome was unconquered.

Now, 600 years later, there were no competent armies facing Alaric. The city was full of soft and wealthy people, an unemployed and unemployable mob living on government handouts, and slaves. No reinforcements were quickly available. Alaric had been an officer in the Roman Army. He now wanted to be commander in chief of Roman armed forces. He could fight with them, or against them. It was their choice. The Goths, his Germanic people, had never been really conquered by the Romans. They had through centuries of contact become partly Romanized. They provided the best soldiers to the Roman armies. They were fierce, larger men, and independent in spirit. They were being slowly driven westward by the Huns coming from the east. These were massive movements of whole peoples. Rome had exhausted its military strength by constant warfare and conquest. It was no longer able to defend itself against forces of this magnitude.

The slaves in Rome at night secretly opened one of the city gates. The Goths poured in. They torched the nearby houses to show the way for the rest of their forces, then they pillaged the city for 6 days. Because they were mostly Christians as was Alaric, on his orders they left the churches unharmed and did not massacre or enslave the population, although the slaves took some revenge on their former masters. The Goths just stripped Rome of its wealth and then poured like an incoming tide over the rest of Italy.

Rome was then 1173 years old. It had ceased to be the centre of the empire for some time. Only on 3 occasions in the last 100 years had emperors even visited Rome, and then only briefly. Western emperors lived at Milan or Ravenna; Constantine built his own capital in the east -- Constantinople -- and shifted half the Senate there. For several hundred years there had been military despotism and the Emperor with his ministers ran the state. The Senate at Rome had degenerated into a mixture of country club and municipal council.

It wasn't just the sacking of Rome in 410 AD that ended the Empire. The Visigoths settled in Gaul and Spain. The Vandals crossed to Africa. The Anglo-Saxons invaded Britain. The Huns invaded Italy. Province after province fell to invaders. Then in 455 AD Rome was sacked again, this time by the Vandals. After various nominal emperors came and went,

Orestes made his young son Romulus Augustus emperor, the last emperor of the Roman empire. But Odoacer, a local chieftain, killed Orestes and deposed the child emperor, in 476 AD. The Senate of Rome wrote to Constantinople saying the seat of the universal empire should be transferred from Rome to Constantinople and they renounced the right to choose their own ruler. They requested that Odoacer be given the title of Patrician for the administration of the diocese of Italy.

After more than 2 centuries of widespread political corruption, internal wars, mostly inept government and oppression of the population, Rome, the once proud city and head of the former mighty Roman Empire, had ceased to exist as a political power.

The political aspect of a society is like a framework or skeleton; it should hold the society together and guide it. The military should defend it from predatory attacks of other rapacious societies. So now let's see what happened to the military of Rome during those last eventful years.

THE ARMY
Even in its most successful phase of dominance the Roman army was never really able to conquer the Germanic peoples to the north. But late in the life of Roman society the Germanics as a people were being pushed from the north and east by migrating peoples as fierce or fiercer than they were. The Goths asked for a province within the Empire, and food and subsidy to help their relocation. The long delays, changes of mind, perfidy of Roman ministers and weakness of rulers finally caused the Goths to come and take what they needed by force.

The Roman army in its greatness had always consisted of sturdy citizens well trained in martial arts. Later as the supply dwindled they were replaced by Romanized provincials from

Gaul, Spain, Africa, Illyria, and elsewhere. Even these troops began to dwindle in the last phase of degeneration and decay to the death. The imperial armies probably spent almost as much time fighting one another as they did protecting the borders. There were not now enough forces to do both at once.

One solution was to cut the size of a legion from 6000 men to 1500. Auxiliaries were also decreased in size. Towards the end, an army of three of these legions plus auxiliaries sent north to defend Italy was about 5,000 men, less than a former single legion.

From the time of Commodus to Constantine nearly 100 governors "raised the standard of revolt." To prevent governors from controlling the armies in their provinces and proclaiming themselves emperors, the command was divided. Governors were now civilian officers with civilian staff and the army was a separate command. Unfortunately for Rome this meant slower response time in the event of an attack across the border. The Governor controlled the supplies. Logistically the troops might have negotiations and delays in getting supplies in the right quantities to the right place at the right time. It was Napoleon who said "an army marches on its stomach."

Towards the end, when Julian was in the east, about to fight the King of Kings, Sapor of the Parthians, his men complained they were going to have to fight after receiving a mere 150 pieces of silver as a donation. It was always customary for a Roman commander in chief to give an oration to his assembled troops to stir their courage and intensity before the battle. Here's what Julian is reported to have said,

"Believe me, the Roman Republic which formerly possessed such immense treasures is now reduced to want and wretchedness, our princes and ministers have been purchasing with gold the tranquility of the barbarians. The revenue is exhausted, the cities are ruined, the provinces are dispeopled. The only inheritance I have received from my royal ancestors is a soul incapable of fear...."

The border troops only received about 2/3 of the pay of those close to the imperial government. But the border troops carried the load of defence of the empire. In disaffection they began to side with the "barbarians", share their spoils -- at least look the other way when incursions into imperial territory occurred. The continued and gradual increases in pay helped exhaust the Roman treasury. It became difficult to get youths to take on the hardships and dangers of military service. Slaves were allowed into the ranks and veterans granted leave on condition their sons joined the army. Then came levies on provincials. They had to take up arms or find a substitute or pay a heavy fine; this was reduced to 42 pieces of gold. Some youths in Italy and the provinces cut off fingers from their right hands to avoid military service. This practice is connected with our word 'mutilate'.

The legions had relaxed discipline and being out of condition found the body armour and helmets too heavy to wear. They asked and got permission to leave them off. They didn't like the short sword and spear of their ancestors. But you can't hold a shield when you're using a bow. The emperors could not get the legions to go back to wearing armour. Meanwhile the cavalry of the Goths, Huns and Alemanni had begun to use defensive armour. They were excellent archers and could overwhelm the legions who now had little protection.

With the finest Roman stock long since killed in conquests or civil wars, and brave but less disciplined and poorly trained foreigners fighting Rome's wars, the degenerate society was now less than capable of defending itself.

But there's more to a society than this. It has a financial and economic aspect. Let's see how this ran its course in the final phase of Rome.

FINANCE, ECONOMIC HEALTH AND TAXATION

Some historians have told us high taxation ruined and destroyed the Roman Empire. Even from this brief survey of some major circumstances in the nearly 300 years of the Roman society's decadence into death, we can see there's more to it than that. But the broad financial outline is clear -- first Rome sacked and pillaged the wealthy cities and societies surrounding it. Then it squandered the proceeds in luxury living and buying off less "civilized" peoples who attacked it. As the money and wealth supplies dwindled, taxes went up, and the coinage was debased until 98% of the coinage was base metal. Finally, money became scarce and little used; the citizens were now bartering goods and services directly and probably escaping some taxation in the process -- an underground economy had grown. Because of the shortage of coinage in circulation, commerce was stifled. Salaries began to be paid in food and clothing, taxes were collected in produce.

The Catholic church was becoming a large and wealthy institution. It was receiving funds from the state and from private individuals, building up a treasury within the state. By the time Attila the Hun descended on Rome it was not an emperor but the Supreme Pontiff of the Catholic Church that arranged the payment of gold to buy him off. This gradual creation of a wealthy state within a state was siphoning off financial resources that formerly were available to the empire for its own use. A church does not produce goods and tangible services.

Many of the emperors in this last phase of the Roman Society taxed their citizens mercilessly. Taxation of citizens became so extreme that Lactantius said there were more people collecting taxes than there were paying them. Laws were passed binding the peasants "to the soil" and compelling a town man to follow the occupation of his father. Deprived of their freedom, people sank into wretchedness and despair. This helped the spread of Christianity and oriental religions of passivity, other worldliness; man could give up the hopeless struggle in this world and hope for reward in a life after death.

The unjust taxation, especially of the merchant and middle class, discouraged the development of new economic ventures. A substantial bureaucracy grew up in finance and administration headed by the master of the offices. Beginning with 200 - 300 messengers to carry edicts and official news to the provinces, these messengers gradually came to report back on what they saw, and became the spies of the emperor and scourge of the people. Their numbers grew to over 10,000. Then they either solicited bribes or reported citizens as treasonable. The wealthy risked incrimination, torture, loss of property and death.

Each year an 'indiction' written in purple ink in the hand of the emperor went out to the provinces within two months of Sept. 1 prescribing the tribute based on budget requirements. If revenue was down or expenses higher an additional 'superindiction' was imposed. As well, there was tribute in kind for the land. A census every 15 years revalued the properties for tax purposes. On the evidence of an actual survey an exception was granted for 330,000 acres of prime land in Italy, now deserted and uncultivated. This was before the attacks of the predatory border peoples, so presumably over- taxation and civil wars had ruined it.

The assessment was levied on a province divided by the number of heads (a capitation or poll tax). Constantine levied 25 pieces of gold for the annual tribute of every head in Gaul, one of the richest provinces. This conduct of affairs exhausted it. His successor reduced the levy to 7 pieces of gold. Several indigent citizens had to group together to form a "head". A wealthy provincial in proportion to his fortune had to contribute a number of "heads". Apparently the Roman levies on Gaul were about 4 times those on pre-revolutionary France in the 1700s AD in the same geographic area.

As losses of provinces occurred the revenue and strength of the Empire diminished. When Sapor took 5 wealthy provinces in the east with 3 fortress cities, this was a severe shock to the finances and spirit of the Roman Empire. One ancient writer said the prisoners, scribes and fugitives formed the greatest part of the inhabitants.

The assessment procedure for taxation devolved down to the municipalities where the councillors were personally responsible for making up any deficit. Property owners had to be councillors. This caused such a tax burden that property owners avoided public office at all costs, even abandoning their lands and going to other cities to find employment. If caught they were brought back and forced to suffer the tax consequences.

The denarii were small value Roman coins. In
302 AD there were 50,000 denarii to a pound of gold
334 AD there were 300,000 denarii to a pound of gold
337 AD. . . . . 20,000,000 denarii to a pound of gold
357 AD. . . . . . . 330,000,000 denarii to a pound of gold.

This statistic alone shows us the extent of inflation in 60 years or so and the financial and monetary instability suffered by Roman citizens shortly before the death of the Rome society.

A society also has beliefs, laws and a justice system, social conditions and health, and finally it is subjected to natural events; plagues, famines, droughts, earthquakes, floods, and so on. Let's look at the beliefs of Rome in its last phase. I suggest we should then have given ourselves a sufficient perspective to see how Rome declined to its death without considering any further aspects of its demise.

BELIEFS

Apparently humans are prepared to die in large numbers for their beliefs. A general discussion of the impact of beliefs on the lives of societies will come later, but for now we will just look at the Roman Society and its beliefs. Worship of the Immortals with idols and sacrifices had been the established religion of many societies in the Mediterranean civilization for thousands of years. It was the fate of Roman Society to experience the onset of Christianity. It began its phase of decline and death with the state religion of the Immortals. Before its death this had been banned and Christianity, or rather Catholicism, had become the mandatory state religion. The transition was turbulent. As Jesus is quoted in Matthew 10:34-5 of the New Testament of the Bible (King James Version):

"Think not that I am come to send peace on earth: I have not come to send peace, but a sword. For I am come to set a man at variance against his father and the daughter against her mother....",

Faith in the religion of the Immortal gods was declining by the time of Plato in ancient Greece. Gradually Zoroastrianism, Mithraism, Stoicism, each in turn moved more towards a personal conception of "god". Then in the declining phase of Rome Neo-Platonism was popular. This had degenerated into little more than fake mysticism and magic. The strength of belief in the old Immortal religion had gone completely, only the practice and form of it remained .

Into this vacuum the arrival of the ideas of Jesus of Nazareth was electrifying. We can best understand this by seeing the modern belief engendered by Karl Marx and his Communist Manifesto in 1848 which ended: "Working men of the world, unite". Within 150 years this doctrine had caused many revolutions and took hold as a government in Russia and China, two of the largest nations on this planet, one in contiguous territory, the other in population..

No record has been found in Roman history to substantiate the biblical tale of the life of Jesus of Nazareth. His birth is thought by some modern scholars to have been about 4 BCE, to fit more closely with a known Roman census, than the choice of 1 AD by the Catholic church

.

Believers in the old established Immortals religion thought the Christians were atheists. Although the Christians were a troublesome sect, the Romans tried to avoid persecuting them. Diocletian had 4 eunuchs as assistants. They were all Christians. But Galerius was a strong believer in the old religion and was involved in the destruction of churches and 'martyrdom' of Christians. Just before he retired Diocletian did issue edicts against Christians but Constantine, who followed him, favoured them and ameliorated the edicts.

In 321 AD (AD being Anno Domini, Latin for 'the year of our Lord') by the Edict of Milan Constantine ordered the churches as places of worship to be restored without dispute or delay, if any purchaser paid a fair price to be indemnified from the imperial treasury. There was tolerance of all religions including Christianity. But Lucinius in the east went back on this and dismissed Christians from his service. By the mid 350s AD the Catholic church had 1800 bishops. These were now to be tried by their peers and ecclesiastical law came into being. The ancient privilege of sanctuary was transferred to Christian churches.

In AD 325 the Emperor convened at Nice in Bithynia an assembly to decide the dispute over the Trinity. 318 bishops attended and 2048 of other ranks and sects. Constantine, the Emperor, frequently attended. He gave the clergy security, wealth, and power. Support of the orthodox faith was now considered the most sacred duty of the civil magistrate. The Edict of Milan which confirmed to each individual the privilege of choosing his own religion soon degenerated into disagreements with the 'orthodox' meaning 'against the emperor's commands' and so heresy and punishable-- the property of heretics was confiscated for the emperor and the church. Before Constantine condemned the Manichaeans (as a heresy) he commissioned a civil magistrate to make an accurate enquiry into the nature of their religious principles. As a result he exempted the Novations from penalties of the law. There was a Donatist faction. They claimed apostolic succession was interrupted in Europe and Asia, but not by them in Africa. Other schisms were Arianism, the Gnostics and the Ebronites. The early theologian Athanasius said of the Trinity the more he thought about it, the less he comprehended it. He is not alone, it was a compromise solution. It doesn't make sense to philosophers or logicians.

The Christians inflicted more martyrdom on themselves than they suffered from the Romans. 5 times Athanasius was expelled from his throne as archbishop of Alexandria, primate of Egypt. The Synod of Tyre with Arians strong in the east, condemned him. 2 bishops contended for the 'episcopal throne', one, Paul, a Nicene creed follower, was driven from the throne several times, finally strangled by order of Philip, a principal minister of the emperor Constantius who appointed Macedonius (an Arian) In Paul's place. The people disputed this, took up arms and the consecrated ground was their field of battle. The well before the church overflowed with blood. Macedonius was determined to stamp out those not Arians. He sent 4000 regular troops to Phamphlagoria. The locals with scythes and axes left almost the entire 4000 dead, although many locals died also. While "the flames of the Arian Controversy consumed the vitals of the Empire" the Christian Donatists rebelled in Africa. "The kingdom of heaven through the enmity of Christians for one another turned into chaos or hell itself".

The sons of Constantine shut down the non-Christian temples "It is our pleasure that in all places in all cities the temples be immediately shut". Apparently this was not well enforced as the temples continued in existence. The divisions among the Christians helped delay the ruin of the Immortals religion.

The emperor Julian was brought up as a Christian but in the midst of the (eastern) Arian controversy, Christian dogma and infighting didn't impress him. He reformed the ancient religion. Platonists in his time had moved the old religion from belief in physical Immortals to belief that they existed in the heavens and the soul of man could disengage from its material bonds and reunite with the infinite divine spirit.

An edict of Julian gave free and equal religious toleration for all citizens whatever their faith, but Christians were not to stigmatize their fellow subjects as idolators and heretics. The old religion was to open all its temples. The bishops and clergy banished by the Arians were now restored. Julian gave orders before his death to restore the temple of Jerusalem. He transferred back to the older religion allowances from public revenue granted by Constantine or his sons to Christians who were now required to make full restitution for temples they destroyed in the previous reign.

George of Cappodocia "born in a fullers shop" made a fortune selling bacon to the army. He rose to be archbishop of Egypt. He impoverished the people with his pomp, and monopoly of nitre, salt, pepper, funerals, and other items. When Julian became emperor George and his master of the mint were dragged in chains to prison and after 24 days the people , impatient of legal justice, broke in and killed them.

Because of constant disorders between Christians themselves and others in the Odessa area, Julian confiscated the whole property of the church there, distributed the money to the soldiers, and the land to the domain of the government. "They will advance with more diligence in the paths of virtue and salvation when they are relieved by my assistance from the load of temporal possessions"....

Two bishops fought over the episcopal seat of Rome. 137 dead bodies were found in the Basilica of the loser. The successful candidate could be sure of enrichment by the offerings of the wealthy matrons of Rome.

Theodosius was the first emperor baptized in the "true faith of the Trinity" AD 380. In 15 years Theodosius promulgated at least 15 edicts against heretics, including a fine of 10 lbs. of gold on any one who should promote an heretical ordination. The Arian belief was that the Son was inferior to the Father. My own reading of only the words of the New Testament attributed directly to Jesus indicates that his position was that he was 'the son of man', was a messenger and had the task of delivering the message first to Jews, then to Gentiles. This type of statement is repeated a number of times. Only once is he reported to have said he was the Son of God and since this is inconsistent with the other statements I suspect it is a copyist's addition to enhance the image. Such 'inflations' were not unknown among hand copyists in the centuries before printing presses. However, the Council of Constantinople in 381 established the Trinity with 3 equal deities, the Father, Son and Holy Ghost or Spirit. Typical of the perversity of humans, the 'Son of man' who came with a message from 'God the Father' had his message largely ignored and was now himself worshipped as a God.

At age 34, before he was baptized, Ambrose, a consular whose jurisdiction included Milan and the Imperial residence, was transferred from governor to archbishop. Gratian, the then western emperor loved and revered him. In a small town near the Persian border a bishop and his adherents burned a Jewish synagogue. The local magistrate ordered them to rebuild it or repay the damage. The eastern emperor, Theodorus, confirmed this. Ambrose was against it, as a persecution of the Christian religion. He caused Theodorus to cancel the restitution order.

Theodosius gave orders to prohibit the use of sacrifices, shut the temples and confiscate the consecrated property for the benefit of the emperors, the church and the army. Christian zealots led by bishops in east and west tore down the temples, some with difficulty. The archbishop of Alexandria, Theophilus, caused the destruction of pagan temples there and apparently also the library of Alexandria. Theodosius then passed a law that worshipping an idol by sacrifice of guiltless victims and divination was a crime of high treason against the state. But the believers in the old religion weren't persecuted, many were still in public service.

By now the worship of "saints" and "relics" had begun to corrupt the simplicity and purity of the original message of Jesus. An ecclesiastical hierarchy had already entrenched itself. I suggest organized religion had become a product of the intellect, was materialistic and used belief as an instrument of power.At the fall of Rome Gothic Christians were fighting Gothic Christians and despoiling Roman Christians which seems to have little to do with the original message of the Sermon on the Mount or even the Old Testament 10 commandments.

So now we have seen evidence for the decay of Rome's political system, its army, its economic and financial strength and even its beliefs. The death of Rome and its Empire was a natural consequence.

VENICE
We discussed the decline and death of Venice in chapter 4. It seems unnecessary to repeat the unfolding of events that led to its demise.
The decline and death of the two societies occurred as:
Rome: . . 180 - 476 = 296 years
Venice: 1574 - 1787 = 223 years.

We can see that the sack of Rome in 410 gives a 7 year difference from Venice. The additional 66 years before final expiry of Rome occurred because it was a huge society in what I have called the Mediterranean civilization and did not succumb immediately as did Venice.

I suggest to you that the similarities between the final phase of these two very different societies, Rome and Venice, are so close as to justify my view that what we have here is the life history of two living social organisms. If we agree on this, now we're ready to see where this conclusion leads us.

SECTION 3

CHAPTER 11
WHY DO SOCIETIES FIGHT?

CHAPTER 12
TRADE AND THE LIFE CYCLE OF SOCIETIES

CHAPTER 13
IDEAS

CHAPTER 14
APPLYING THE THEORY
GERMANY AND RUSSIA

CHAPTER 15
IS OUR CIVILIZATION DYING?

CHAPTER 11

WHY DO SOCIETIES FIGHT

There are today only about 170 independent nations on this planet but since World War II there have been over 150 wars around the world. What is the relationship of war to a society? Wars have been analyzed by the mathematically minded as to their frequency, graded by their size, the number of nations involved, the number of participants, the number of casualties. For example, as you go down the scale of frequency of involvement Richardson has found from 1820 AD to 1945 first China, then Turkey and then Britain in that order. And Quincey Wright found in a much longer period from 1550 to 1900, analyzed into 50-year periods, first in each period was France, then Spain, then Britain, then Britain, then Russia, then Britain and then Britain. Such information is interesting but has not told us why wars are fought.

Contemporary psychologists and philosophers have turned their attention to the problem of cooperation. If there is cooperation there is no conflict. What are the principles underlying cooperation? One famous problem dealing with cooperation is known as the Prisoner's Dilemma. That's because the original version related to two prisoners. Let's make up a simplified version and try it out on you.

Suppose you have plenty of wood, and your neighbour John has crops of grain. Each of you wants some of what the other has, and you arrange to trade fixed amounts monthly. But you each have to drop your goods off at a location on the other's land not knowing what the other has left in exchange, and you never meet. For the first exchange should you leave the agreed amount, or nothing, hoping to go to John's lot and pick up the first load of grain and so gain an advantage. Logically, if you do this and there is nothing for you, you have lost nothing, and if the load is there you have gained something for nothing. But John will have the same thoughts. If both of you leave nothing, logically, neither has lost on the deal, but you could each have had a lasting benefit with what you wanted if you had 'cooperated' and not 'defected'. If both you and John bring full loads the first month, what will you do the next month, and so on. Collectively, you would be better off by cooperating, but as 'egoists' acting logically you might decide to 'defect', each trying to win an advantage.

From our point of view one particular Prisoner's Dilemma experiment is very interesting because a fully cooperative person who was a pacifist by nature cooperated at every move in full expectation that the other player would cooperate. But in this case, throughout the entire course of the experiment the other player did not once change his strategy, and instead of seeing the long term advantage of cooperating, from the beginning to end took advantage of the pacifically minded player, and apparently considered him naive or foolish. The experimenter noted that this was a traumatic experience for this particular believer in non-violence. I'm sure you can see the relevance of this to the problem of relationships between nations, armaments and disarmament, and therefore national security of a society and the problem of war.

But thousands of years before our contemporary psychologists were experimenting with the "Prisoner's Dilemma", Phoenicians, the Mediterranean civilization's greatest sea peoples, were trading with north African peoples. Neither could speak the language of the other. The Phoenicians would come ashore, lay out on the beach the items they were prepared to trade, then retreat back to sea again. The North African people would come down to the beach, look over what was there, take what they wanted, and replace it with items they were willing to provide in exchange. Then they would withdraw and the Phoenicians came back, took what they wanted of what was left for them plus their own goods not taken, and sailed away.

We did not find in the whole life cycle of Venice that it acted altruistically to help a friendly state. It obtained trading privileges for any assistance it gave, fought many wars, had few allies and always appeared to act in what it considered its best self interest. Rome apparently behaved in the same way. In all that we noted of Rome's life span we did not once come across a treaty of friendship with another society, although conquered societies were sometimes required to support Rome as allies in the future.

By the time of the middle ages in our Western civilization kings ruling societies would often arrange royal marriages to try to cement friendly relationships with other societies. This only worked when the societies themselves had a common interest.

Computers are now generally used in war strategies and in war 'games'. Computer analysts have developed what is now called game theory. Don't be misled by the word game. It doesn't mean 'play' but strategic theory worked out in simulated form on computers. For example, political scientist Robert Axelrod invited a number of game theorist professionals, and academics who had published studies on the logic of the problem of cooperation, to compete in a round-robin tournament to see which computer encoded strategy could best respond to the Cooperation or Defection of all other entrants. 15 programs were entered. The shortest was 4 lines, Tit for Tat, by Anatol Rapoport of the University of Toronto. The longest was 77 lines. One entry, Random, merely 'flipped a coin' so to speak. Tit for Tat began by cooperating and then it merely repeated the other player's previous move. If the other player defected, then it defected in its next move, and so on. It never provoked a breakdown of mutual trust, but it replied in kind to a punitive act. Tit for Tat won the contest.Dr. Axelrod then solicited entries from around the world for a more sophisticated contest. 63 strategies were submitted, the longest being 152 lines from New Zealand. World experts on game theory competed this time, but Tit for Tat, the shortest, simple 4 line program, won again.

Computer game theory doesn't tell us why societies fight, but suggests that the best strategy for survival is not to attack, but always to reply in kind to an attack. This seems quite similar to the foreign policy of Israel in the late 20th century.

So why do societies fight? Here's a cameo example. The Suez canal, passing through Egyptian territory, joins the Mediterranean sea with the Indian Ocean. It was built by a French corporation, completed in 1869. The Egyptian ruler was near bankruptcy and sold all his shares in the Canal to Britain in 1875, for 4 million pounds. That was about half the total shares outstanding.

The Ottoman Empire (Turkey) sided with Germany in World War I (1914-1918) and so lost most of its possessions at the end of the war, including Egypt. In 1914 a British protectorate was set up in Egypt. During World War 2 there was fighting nearby between British, German and Italian forces. A republic was proclaimed in Egypt in 1953 . In 1956 General Nasser became president and British troops were withdrawn from the Suez canal. A month later Egypt announced nationalization of the Canal. Britain and France landed forces and attacked Egypt. They intended to take back their rights to the Canal. The US told them to stop it and go home, which they then did. So why did these societies fight? Because they had perceived infringement of their interests. Societies can do what they like unless there's someone to stop them.

DOES WAR KILL A SOCIETY?
We saw how Venice died, through internal collapse because it knew resistance to Napoleon's declaration of war was hopeless, and death when Napoleon stripped it. But is it really war that kills a society? Let's look at a living society: Germany today.

In the 20th century Germany was defeated in World War I, was forced into paying 'reparations' and suffered hyperinflation (with trillion mark bank notes) and virtual national bankruptcy.

It lost its colonial empire. It was defeated again in World War II and suffered severe manpower losses. Some of its cities were more or less levelled. It was stripped of its rocketry expertise and advanced equipment, it was partitioned and its capital and territory were still occupied over 40 years later. Is it a dead society? Obviously, not.

The answer is that if a 75-year old man is badly beaten and stripped of his possessions he will probably die, but a 30-year old receiving exactly the same treatment will probably survive. The German Mercedes and Porsche have as great or greater reputation and prestige value as any US cars. And the then East Germany, living under a political system which appeared to give little outlet for its talents, in the 1987 world games won 40 gold medals, more than either the US or the USSR, one of the few ways it could express its national identity -- how it did this (apparently by use of banned drugs) is, I suggest not as significant as its determination to express itself nationally as the best.

Japan is a modern example of a society in its phase of expansion. Between 1894 and 1941, a period of less than 50 years, Japan attacked first Russia, then China, then the US. That's 3 major powers, all with much larger populations than Japan's 120 million. But after defeating Russia and China, Japan was finally stopped militarily. The US nuclear attack had a profound effect on the psyche of the Japan society, causing it to create films where monstrous prehistoric creatures hatched from eggs to tear down cities. At the other extreme Japan society avidly took up baseball as a national sport. Since World War 2 Japan has directed its efforts into economic expansion. By 1990 5 of the 10 largest banks in the world were Japanese. Japan has established manufacturing facilities in Canada, the US, Europe and Asia. It is a world leader in technology and has the second largest economy in the world. So, blocked in military expansion it has succeeded in economic expansion and has reached its phase of dominance as a society in this non-militaristic way.

We have evidence, then, that societies in the expansionary phase, if stopped in territorial expansion through warfare continue to expand in other ways. Unless a society is in the decayed stage and is stripped so that it dies, or is deliberately put to death as was Carthage by Rome, we can conclude that wars do not ordinarily kill a society.

THE EF THEORY OF WAR AND SOCIETY

There may be another way to look at this problem of war. If societies have life cycles, as I say they do, then the wars they get into in the various stages of their life cycle may be different.

Societies move through their life cycle in 5 main phases. Wars may accompany each phase. There is a type of war we can call a Phase I war. This arises in the first few hundred years of life of a society when establishing its position. It's a formative war, to secure its existence as a society, Rome fought such wars in its first phase. Its methods were always thorough. It conquered a nearby Etruscan city, Falerii, that it thought threatened it. Then Rome systematically destroyed it, and moved the inhabitants to another site, Falerii Nova, which was on a plain and indefensible. That is a calculated protective act of a society in its formative phase.

Phase II wars are wars of ascendancy. The society is now fighting its neighbours to establish and secure its place in its civilization, obtain defensible frontiers and sustainable resources and absorb when it can weaker neighbours which seem to be in its way.

Phase III wars are wars of expansion. A society is now expanding through its trade, its beliefs, its message, its cultural identity. Expansion may be by armed conflict overpowering others to create colonies, but can be by Christian missionaries, Marxist adherents, McDonald's (25,000 restaurants in 114 countries), acquisition by multi-national corporations, and so on. This is the phase of colonization at a distance, beyond its boundaries. It may lead to cannibalistic wars, wars of unnecessary over-expansion. In time the society finds it easier to go on taking from others than pursuing its own productivity, which brought it to power. It has permeated the areas it has reached and seems to be unable to stop the process of conquest. Venice in this phase digested the spoils of Byzantium, and Rome digested Britain and Egypt. (Venice and Rome were each about 800 years old at the time.) These wars continue into the phase of dominance.

Phase IV wars begin to occur during the mid to late stages of the phase of dominance. They are merely actions as necessary to ensure the dominance is maintained.

Phase V wars begin to occur during the last stages of the phase of dominance of a society. They are defensive wars against extinction. In some cases they are initiated by less sophisticated, less enervated, less exhausted and less wealthy societies or groups which have not yet coalesced into mature societies, but are in their formative or ascendancy phase. These wars occur when a society in the phases of growth crosses paths with a society in its declining phase. For example, the expanding Turks moved into the territory of the declining Venice. These defensive wars continue during the decline and decay of a society and usually end with its final defeat and demise.

TESTING THE THEORY IN PRACTICE
Let's try our theory on a recent example of war. We'll take a simple case: the Falklands war. The Falklands, or Malvinas, are about 400 miles (700 km) off the coast of Argentina, close to 8,000 miles (13,000 km) from Britain. Population of the islands about 2,000, 97% English speaking settlers. The English apparently settled there in 1766, Britain took possession in 1834.

SOUTH AMERICAN SOCIETIES

Brazil is the largest society in South America. Argentina is the second largest. Brazil has a population of over 150 million, larger than all the other South American societies put together, including Argentina. Brazil's land area is almost as great as the rest of South America, including Argentina.

Argentina, Brazil, Paraguay and Uruguay are neighbours. Argentina and Brazil each have borders with the other three. Both Paraguay and Uruguay have borders with their two large neighbours, but not with each other.

Brazil is Portuguese speaking, the others are Spanish. Buenos Aires, now capital of Argentina, was Spanish, but soon had a strong Portuguese element. About 97 % of all four societies are practising or non practising Catholics. Since their territories are all composed of arable or pasture land or forest with crops and beef exports, you would expect a peaceful co-existence between them. It was Jesus himself, the founder of their religion, who is reported to have said one of the two great commandments on which "hang all the law and the prophets" is "Love thy neighbour as thyself" (Matthew 22.39) and "turn the other cheek" to enemies.(Matthew 5.39) Such is not the case here among these devout Catholics as we will soon see.

All four got their independence, from Portugal (Brazil) and Spain (Argentina and Paraguay) thanks to the Napoleonic wars. Then Uruguay obtained its independence from Brazil in 1828. Civil wars raged there until 1865.

ARGENTINA
The territory which later became Argentina was first invaded by the Spanish in about 1513-14. But settlement began in about 1536. In 1810 there was a revolt against Spanish rule. In 1816, again thanks to Napoleon, the "United Provinces" declared their independence. But Buenos Aires refused to join them. It was already a growing city. The United Provinces convened a constituent assembly in 1824 and created the office of President. If we take the creation of the society of

Argentina as about 1536, then the formative phase as ending with a Presidency in 1824, we have 288 years, close to Venice's 276 years, which included the first Doge at 270 years. Argentina was sheltered by and subject to the Spanish empire until it claimed independence.

Now that the provinces had coalesced there was an immediate 3 year war by the fledgling Argentina against Brazil (1825-8).

Remarkably, apparently Brazil was defeated. Next, there was a war with Buenos Aires (1859-61). After that Buenos Aires joined the United Provinces in 1862. Argentina in conjunction with its two neighbours now embarked on a 5 year war against Paraguay (1865 to 1870). Almost all Paraguay's male population was lost, its total population dropped from about 450,000 to 220,000. Paraguay also lost 60,000 square miles of territory. It was the only one of the four without a seacoast.

Following that war Argentina turned inwards to war with its interior indigenous peoples until they were 'subdued' to use the language of historians and military strategists.

Between about 1850 and 1930 Argentina had to cope with massive immigration from Italy and Spain, said to total about 30% of its population. From 1946 the Perons were in power and on their deaths there were civil wars between their supporters and the military. It's said about 20,000 perished in these conflicts. All these military activities after the end of the formative phase are characteristic of an ascendancy phase which, having lasted only 158 years by 1982 is apparently far from over. And in 1982 Argentina with a population of about 30 million, invaded the Falkland Islands.

Argentina is probably moving towards the end of its ascendancy phase and nearer the beginnings of the expansionist phase, a phase usually involving external wars and internal unrest as the society struggles to establish itself and chart a course for expansion from the location it finds itself in, using the resources available to it. We have seen from our examples that regrettably a society in its ascendancy phase will attack any other society that stands in its path of expansion, even if that territory is occupied by a much larger and far more powerful society. So for Argentina the Falklands war was a phase II or ascendancy war.

BRITAIN
Now let's look at Britain's side of the war. Unfortunately for Argentina, Britain had claimed the islands 148 years previously, and by 1982 there were about 2,000 British settlers there comprising almost the entire population. The principal occupation is sheep grazing and wool processing. The major trading partners are Britain, the Netherlands and Japan, not South America. Britain was not going to allow its citizens to be overrun without support from the mother country and so found itself unwillingly dragged into a war.

Britain is a complex society with a population close to 60 million, but after World War I it began the slow wind down from Phase IV to Phase V. So for Britain the Falklands war is a Phase IV or defensive war.

In this particular instance Britain, close to 1,100 years old but still the 3rd largest naval power in the world, was able, though at a great distance, to push the 450 year old invading society back from the Falklands. There was much publicity in Britain as to the great cost of the war and that the defence of the Falklands would have to continue as a much higher expense than formerly.

Britain used the same strategy as Tit for Tat. It pushed the invading society out of the disputed area but made no attempt to attack the society itself. Nor did the invading society attempt to attack Britain elsewhere.

INTERNAL WARS

So far we've only mentioned external wars, but can civil wars and rebellions tell us something about the phase a society has reached and the condition it's in? Let's select 4 societies to check on this phenomenon: Canada, the US, Britain, and Venice. Here are the results in schematic form. The numbers give the approximate age of the society in years at the time of the occurrence:

CANADA	USA	BRITAIN	VENICE
230 (1)	260 (4)	340 (6)	350 (11)
270 (2)	370 (5)	415 (7)	550 (12)
330.(3)		600 - 700 (8)	900 (13)
		850 (9)	
		1100 (10)	

CANADA
(1) Papineau in Quebec; William Lyon Mackenzie in Toronto (rebellions)
(2) Red River (Manitoba) rebellion; Northwest rebellion (1885)
(3) Regina Riots; On to Ottawa Trek

USA
(4) Civil War (North vs South)
(5) Watts Riots, Los Angeles, (1965)
. . . Detroit and Newark race riots (1967)
. . . Kent State, Ohio, and National Guard (1970)

BRITAIN
(6) Civil war: Stephen & Matilda
(7) Magna Carta
(8) A century of internal strife. Eg. Jack Cade's rebellion (in Kent): York vs. Lancaster: Simnel: Warbeck: Cornish uprising.
(9) Cromwell
(10) Poll tax riots (1990)

VENICE
(11) Civil uprising: partisans of Franks vs. Partisans of Byzantines

(12) Uprising. Palace burned, Doge murdered
(13) popular revolt, 10 years later a patricians revolt.

All this is interesting but no regular pattern is discernible. What does lie behind it then? One thing we notice is that the same period, 1400s to 1500s AD, when Britain was 600 - 700 years old, was a similar period of internal upheaval in central Europe. The Hussites were fighting and defeating their government, there were wars between towns and princes, there were peasant rebellions in various places.

The Hussite movement may give us a clue. John Huss was a follower and friend of Wycliffe. This was the beginning of the religious (Protestant) reformation movement. It spread across the societies of Europe, the Western civilization, and was a war of ideas, a rising movement of change in patterns of thought. There were empathetic leaders in various societies more or less at the same time. The dates, as usual, are approximations:

NAME	SOCIETY	ACTIVE
Calvin	France	1535
Erasmus	Dutch	1520
Huss	Bohemia	1410
Luther	Germanic	1530
Wycliffe	English	1370
Zwingli	Swiss	1520

If we are right about this, can we find it occurring again at another time, with new ideas? I think we can: 1848, the year of revolutions, the year Marx and Engels published their Communist Manifesto, reflecting the ferment of the age. There were revolutions or uprisings in Baden, Berlin, Cracow, Dresden, Hungary, Milan, Paris (France became a Republic), Parma, Prague, Sicily, Venice, and Vienna.

So we conclude civil war doesn't have the same origins as external war. Civil war is connected with the spread of new ideas or frustration at excessive government oppression, for example by over-taxation or religious persecution. Internal conflict in a society relates to the ferment of new ideas as societies pass from age to age.

CONCLUSIONS ABOUT THE ROLE OF WAR

We've seen that in our own time Germany and Japan have been deflected from expansion by armed conflict into economic expansion. But in each case this was not voluntary but was accomplished after war with much personal injury, and great loss of life and property. Adolf Hitler may not have conquered the world but his German 'people's car' the Volkswagen Beetle certainly did, and Volkswagen at the end of the century is one of the largest car manufacturers in the world. Two generations after World War 2, Sony of Japan had certainly conquered the world of media equipment.

Wars are very prevalent. They can accompany the self-interested activity of a society in each phase of its life cycle.
There are no practical restraints on the actions of a society other than by violence against it. Economic sanctions have not been particularly successful. NATO was only able to cause Serbia to desist from apparent genocide in Kosovo by intensive air attack on Serbia which seems a very tardy and primitive approach by large societies against a small one. The destruction of Kosovo was not prevented, Serbia suffered significant destruction in retaliation and the leadership of Serbia, responsible for the attack on Kosovo, remains in power. Evidently we have a great deal to learn about societies and how to civilize their behaviour.

If war is a concomitant in the growth of a society and not a motivating force, what is? In the next chapter we'll look at another primary part of a society -- its industry, trade and commerce -- to see if we can better identify what drives a society to cause its rise and then its downfall.

CHAPTER 12

TRADE AND THE LIFE CYCLE OF SOCIETIES

HOW POWERFUL IS EXTERNAL ECONOMIC PRESSURE?
If we want to find out whether the economic factors of industry, trade and commerce can have a life and death effect on a society we have a good test case in 1987-9 with Panama vs. The USA.

Panama, a republic, has a population of about 2 million, in an area smaller than Nova Scotia in Canada, slightly larger than the state of West Virginia in the US. Panama has oil refining, international banking, crops such as bananas and pineapples, some copper, mahogany forests, and fishing. About half its work force is in agriculture and fisheries, the other half in industry and commerce. About half its imports and exports are to the US. Its currency is closely tied in with the US dollar. Because of easy financial and shipping regulations, Panama has considerable merchant marine tonnage registered and substantial international banking. In 1903 Panama granted to the US occupation and control of the Canal zone; in 1977 a new treaty arranged gradual take-over by Panama and withdrawal of US troops by 1999.

By 1987 General Noriega had risen to a position of dominance in the government of Panama. It was alleged in the US that the General had been involved in drug trafficking into the US, and the US government wanted him removed from office.

To accomplish this the US put economic pressure on Panama, for example, by causing US corporations there to make payments to the US government in escrow instead of to the government of Panama.The banks in Panama were closed for weeks. More US troops were shipped into the Canal zone. Businesses shut their doors. The general was then indicted in the US on narcotics charges. But General Noriega did not leave, and his government remained in power. Almost a year later the General was still in office and the US was still unable to dislodge him.

In May 1989 General Noriega annulled election results that showed him losing and he became a dictator. After one unsuccessful coup attempt in October 1989 the US invaded Panama on December 20, captured Noriega and took him to Miami to stand trial on narcotics charges.

I think we have to agree that one of the most powerful economic societies in our present day was unable by purely economic means to force its will on one of the puniest societies in the world today. Similarly the US found it necessary to replace economic sanctions with use of air power to discourage the perceived pretensions of Libya and later, on a larger scale, Iraq.

We can expand our examples of economic sanctions. These were tried in the days of the League of Nations in the 1930s and again more recently in the case of South Africa. The ability of Castro's Cuba to withstand US economic pressure has become almost legendary. So far none of these attempts has achieved its objective -- to force a particular line of conduct on another society and cause a change of government. External trade is apparently so much a part of the life of a society that it cannot just be choked off by economic action of certain other societies, but will find a way to continue. Apparently any effect of economic sanctions was felt most by the poorest section of a society and least by its government. It seems reasonable to conclude that economic pressure put on a society, even on a very small one by a much larger one, cannot of itself bring down a government, and certainly not an entire society.

THE ECONOMY WITHIN A SOCIETY
It has been said that in the earlier more repressive past of the Soviet Union the underground market was as great as 30% of the gross national product, and in Italy the black market is said to have been about 30% in the 1980s. So the natural tendency

within a society is to trade, and if governments over-tax or prohibit certain trade for policy reasons, or are unable to enforce effectively their laws regarding trade, their restrictions are likely to be sidestepped by the will of the society.

DOES THE RISE AND FALL OF TRADE CAUSE THE RISE AND FALL OF A SOCIETY?

I'd like to tell you about the Canadian subsidiaries of four small international corporations that came to my firm for auditing services, within a few years of one another. All four were European, two were German, two were British. All four had the same general purpose. They had been impressed by American technology and the enormous size of the North American consumer market. They thought a subsidiary in Canada would pave the way to breaking into this rich American market.

The Germans exercised extremely strict control over their new subsidiaries. They used state of the art direct communications technology. Head Office in Germany required a copy of every invoice, many detailed reports on prescribed forms, the stockrooms had tight inventory controls, were properly fenced off and locked. The parent company required additional occasional surprise special in-depth investigative audits. The Chairman of the parent Board came each year from Europe and required a detailed personal report from his auditors in addition to the audited annual financial statements. Their businesses prospered, they attacked the American market with confidence and energy and now their network in Canada and the US is almost as big as in Europe. They have subsidiaries in many nations around the world, including Japan.

The British companies left things more or less to their appointees in Canada, just paid the bills and absorbed the losses. Their equipment was not really rugged enough to face

American competition. They never did break into the US market and had less than marginal success in Canada. They found it easier to do business in Africa. After a few years both companies folded their subsidiaries and left Canada.

Four is a very small sample, but I think the results are indicative. It was not just that the mini-colonizations of one society failed, it was their method and their merchandise that failed to take hold. I think this supports my view that Britain is in what I have called Phase 4, the declining phase and approaching Phase 5.

Let's take one more example from business: Honda. Honda has set up a manufacturing facility near the small town of Alliston, Ontario. It has become a big employer there. It has gone out of its way to make friends with the local population which was based mainly on potato farming. Honda brought in its nationals for top management and its state of the art engineering techniques. It has trained local personnel in its ways. It has arranged the setting up of another dedicated subsidiary for parts supplies and a further supplier partially owned. Honda is not resented in the area, but appears to be respected and appreciated for the capital investment it has made and the employment and increased business life it has brought to the area. Here then is a successful mini-colony. It has a first class product and by its presence is upgrading local Canadian know-how and employment, and contributing to an increase in the gross national product.

We began by asking does the rise and fall of its trade cause the rise and fall of a society. My own conclusion from the evidence is that it's the other way around. The rise or fall of a society causes the success or failure of its industry, trade and commerce.

DOES THE TYPE OF GOVERNMENT AFFECT THE TRADE OF A SOCIETY?

If we look at the governments of Carthage, Rome, Byzantium, Venice, Britain, Germany, the US, Canada, Japan and Hong Kong, we see no two are alike. The most successful societies, and here we mean the most powerful economically, seem to have prospered because their government at the time was either composed of the trading class or ruled with a light hand sympathetic to it, and avoided over-taxation or policies detrimental to business. We saw this particularly in the case of the ascendancy of Venice and Hong Kong. The present rate of income taxation in Hong Kong is about half the rate of income taxation in Britain.

The conclusion is that there will be trade, whatever the form of government, but that some attitudes of government encourage trade to prosper, while others depress its energy. This has less to do with the political outlook of a government -- e.g. socialist or capitalist -- than its policies on taxation, employment and trading patterns.

WHAT EFFECT DOES GOVERNMENT ECONOMIC ACTION HAVE ON THE LIFE CYCLE OF A SOCIETY?
The earliest exchange of goods and services was generally by barter. This very early form of trading may even be without the use of language between the parties. And there is of course no government interference in trading at that level. Later, gold and silver were used as a medium of exchange, and the metal was cut up into various sizes by weight to denote the relative value. This was really the beginning of coinage. So honest weights and measures were very important in early times. And cities established their own coinage, some more highly regarded by traders than others.

Down the ages what tended to happen was that goldsmiths and silversmiths who did workmanship in these metals, as their names imply, had quantities of those metals on hand, suitably protected in their strongrooms. Merchants wrote notes to one another, IOUs as it were, saying that the bearer was entitled to so much gold say, from such and such a goldsmith who kept some or all of the merchant's stock of gold. The goldsmiths would also issue their own notes. This was the first stage in banking.

But by say the 18th century AD, governments started to issue paper money and then as so often happens with governments, once they got into the business they monopolized it and made it illegal for anyone else to do it. We can now go all the way to 1922 in the US when the $20. bill said on the face of it in small print "This certifies that there have been deposited in the Treasury of the United States twenty dollars in gold coin, payable to the bearer on demand." You cannot claim the equivalent in gold from any western government today as they have all gone off the gold standard. More than that, by 1999 many major Western Societies have severely reduced their gold reserve: for example, Canada had reduced its gold reserves by 86% in the decade ending in 1999. Instead, governments are increasingly relying on foreign currency reserves. Since all societies now use paper money this is like the proverbial house of cards.

Printing paper money is fine, if you are printing it to replace torn or used paper money that needs replacement, or if you back it with gold or some other real value. But in July 1987 (on national TV news network) the government of Canada was reported to be printing money more than twice as much per person, with twice as much debt, per person, as the United States. All western governments have now printed far more money than they can back with tangible reserves.

When a government, the Canadian government, say, needs money to pay its bills, it can issue a series of bonds, long term or short term, or issue treasury bills - really government IOUs. They're not backed by anything other than the word of the government to repay the money to the lenders on maturity. But shortly before the maturity date the government may see it won't be able to repay these bonds and bills because the costs of its social programs keeps rising, so it creates new issues to have funds to pay off the old issues. Its income for the year is less than the expenses because it owes interest payments on these bonds and bills. Almost half its annual expense is now interest expense, so it increases the number of bonds and bills to cover the shortfall. The deficit it has for the year has to go somewhere so it's added to the national debt. But that increases the amount of interest it has to pay. Now it may find investors are less willing to buy the bonds and bills, so it has to increase the rates of interest it pays on the new issues to encourage people to invest in them.

The government cannot increase the interest rates it pays too far too quickly because the chartered banks who have to deal with the Bank of Canada, the Central Bank, then have to raise their rates. This means businesses and individuals borrowing from the banks have to pay more interest and so they tend to spend less on new vehicles, equipment, buildings, and so on. The economy starts to slow down, money moves more slowly, less revenue comes in for the government which is then either no better off or worse off.

The political party forming the government doesn't want to raise taxes to cover the increased expense because this may cause it to lose the next general election, and once in power any political party wants to stay there and enjoy the benefits.
Another solution for the government is to print more money. That's done by the Bank of Canada in this country. For 1998 (most recent results published) in round numbers for simplicity, and ignoring smaller items and more complicated wording, its balance sheet looks like this (in billions of dollars):

ASSETS

	1998	1997
Due from chartered banks	1	1
Treasury bills.	10	14
Short term bonds.	10	6
Long term bonds	11	9
Total assets	32	30

LIABILITIES

Currency.	32	30

What this seems to tell us is that in 1998 there was a noticeable shift from shorter term to longer term debt and a 2 billion dollar increase in printed currency.

It costs the Bank nothing to print money except printing costs (for designing, and subcontracting costs, or costs of equipment, employees, ink, paper, overhead, and so on), which means what it prints is virtually all profit.

The Central (government owned) Bank 'sells' the paper money to the chartered banks for face value of the currency. It can only 'sell' it to them if the banks need more currency and are willing to buy it, for example around Christmas time. Then the Central Bank may use some of these funds it has created out of paper to buy from the chartered banks some of their treasury bills or bonds or it can buy them from the government itself, in which case it has to pay the government in currency. That's why the Central Bank shows treasury bills and government bonds as its assets, and currency as a liability. It's a liability because if the Chartered banks want to turn in some of their currency to the Central Bank, they can, (say in January) and will get a credit in their account with the Central Bank.

All this is paper representing IOUs to show who owes what to whom. The Central Bank holds in effect nothing but paper in and paper out, said to be 'worth' so much and this is fine while the national economy is growing. But if the economy begins to shrink, then the value of this paper tumbles.

The Central Bank also has a yearly operating statement, in very simplified form it looks something like this (in billions of dollars):

```
Income (interest) . . . . . . .1.8
Expenses. . . . . . . . . . . .0.1
Profit . . . . . . . . . . . . . ... 1.7
Paid to the government.  (1.7)
Retained earnings. . . . .. 0.0
```

That's why the Central Bank doesn't have any capital or retained earnings on its balance sheet. It pays its profit to the government. The interest was received mainly on the government bills and bonds it held.

Governments have habitually overspent. We certainly saw this to be the case with both Venice and Rome in their mature years. And governments devise various ways to create more funds, one popular way through the ages has been by putting more base metal into the coinage. In the 20th century AD a favourite way has been by setting up casinos and lotteries.

In British history most of us are familiar with the marital problems of Henry VIII and his various wives. Henry VIII was also a musician, a poet, a sportsman, and spent money freely. After Henry spent his father's treasury he hit upon the great idea of dissolving the monasteries. They were fairly dissolute by that time, had largely lost the intent of their original saintly purpose and were extremely wealthy. Henry VIII did it in proper fashion. The elderly monks were given life-time pensions and then all the fixed assets, wealth and lands of the monasteries were appropriated. This helped solve the deficit problem in the operation of government.

Now let's come to the present day and the government of Canada. The deficits in the last few years of the 1980s averaged over $30 billion dollars a year. And the change in government in 1984 did not significantly reduce this annual deficit below $30 billion dollars a year. There are about 30 million people in Canada. So that means that for every man woman child and infant in Canada the government every year over-spent more than one thousand dollars. In one year alone a family of four had as its share of the government overspending for that year more than four thousand dollars.

We have to remember that this overspending was taking place when the government was already printing money out of nothing, borrowing money, and operating monopolies. In 1999 the Ontario provincial debt was over $119 billion. The Federal or national debt was over $624 billion. This does not include 'crown corporations' whose accounts are kept separately.
Ontario Hydro Electric, a provincial crown corporation alone owes more than $30 billion in debt. Taking into account all the ten provinces plus the debts of local municipalities and cities the total government debt is probably about a thousand billion dollars. But with only 30 million Canadians, this means that for every man woman child and infant in Canada the governments have run up debts of $33,000 each. In the last thirty years (to 1999) the federal government debt in Canada has risen from about $30 billion to over $624 billion. We're not alone in this. Most western nations are in a similar deficit position, but not so large, proportionately. We have to remember that the government already takes from us by taxation indirectly and directly at all levels of government about 50% or even over 50% of all that we earn.

If you or I were to run into debt in our own lives on this scale, we would immediately be bankrupt. And we shouldn't think that this can't happen to nations. A number of nations have had national bankruptcies, and some more than once.

France was bankrupt in 1720, 1753, 1792 and 1797. We can see that this economic turmoil is tied in with political revolution. Let's look at the 1797 national bankruptcy. The post-1789 revolutionary government issued assignats secured on land seized from the church. This currency, the assignats, could be used by a bearer to buy church land, at which time those assignats were supposed to be retired from circulation by the government, though they could continue in circulation as long as there was land left to be sold. Some people redeemed the notes for land, but the notes were re-issued after land was sold. As more money was needed to prepare for war and satisfy the population, the government kept on printing more notes, creating inflation. Next, prices kept rising, and the government kept printing more money. By 1796 it took 12,000 livres to equal a gold louis, which had once equalled one livre. Although half the church land was sold, the original issue of 400 million livres had climbed to 45.5 billion livres. So the government had resorted to printing paper money without backing. This is clearly a slippery slope, and it led to national bankruptcy.

The most classic case of overprinting money was in Germany at the end of World War I. Immense reparations were demanded by the victors, close to $70 billion. This demand had to be scaled down several times because the German government obviously simply could not pay this kind of amount. There has been considerable retrospective analysis by economists as to exactly what did happen to cause the German mark to collapse as it did. More and more money was printed faster and faster, so fast that at one stage, the backs could not be printed because the ink wasn't drying fast enough to keep up with production requirements. Debtors were chasing creditors, to pay them with now worthless money. Billion mark notes were printed by the end of the collapse of the currency. French troops occupied the Ruhr in January 1923, intending to enforce payment of reparations. The mark had been 20,000 to the dollar, but fell in the next nine months to 4.2 trillion to the dollar. The collapse ended in the next year because the government issued new currency at a trillion to one, and refused to print any more.

It remains something of a mystery how the government got into this predicament and how it was able to extricate itself so firmly.

Within 15 years of the total collapse of the German monetary system a new political order, the Nazi regime, had built a military power which soon overran the rest of continental Europe with remarkable ease and speed. So, after an economic collapse there can be a political revolution which releases great power in the society (as in the Napoleonic and Nazi eras) which shows that the inner strength of the society was there despite economic collapse.

In 1986 Brazil's inflation was said to be 800%. But what happens in hyperinflation, as in Brazil, is that an economic revolution is taking place. It means that the relationship of debtors and creditors in each case is changing and some people who were badly off become much better off and some people who were well off become much more poorly off or are financially ruined. Usually those with fixed incomes or investments (often the elderly) are the ones who suffer most, and those who are earning their income are much better off as wages keep rising.

The interesting thing from our point of view here is that in all the cases we've mentioned, despite economic collapse, all the people in those nations did not suddenly become wiped out. They had to continue to survive, to raise their children, to pay their bills, to earn a living. We can also see that in none of those cases has a society died. The death of Rome, and Inca society, was not economic but political, by military action, although both were incidentally stripped of their economic wealth by the invaders.

PREDICTING THE FUTURE OF AN ECONOMY

Is it possible to predict what an economy will do next, short term or long term?

A short term example is that Mutual Fund managers have habitually underperformed the U.S. or other present day nations' stock market indexes. All an index does is track the performance of a selected group of major stocks being traded. The solution for the Mutual Fund managers has been for their companies to float 'index funds.' With little attempt to manage, these funds merely track the stock market indexes and so generally outperform the managed funds.

A longer term example starts with the economy in Canada in 1958. It began slowing down. Inventories were building up, money was circulating more slowly, people were not paying their bills as promptly as they had been. How did this come about? The reason seemed to be that after WW2 there was a pent-up need by consumers for new equipment, goods and services, but this had largely been satisfied by 1958. Consumers were now more selective in what they bought, there were new, interesting and cheap products coming in from Pacific Rim states, in competition with local manufacture. This seemed quite similar to the situation after WW1. Then it took 11 years from the end of the war before the crash of 1929 and subsequent 'depression'

It was 13 years since the end of WW2 in 1958. There was a north American precedent in what Americans called the 'Panic' of 1819, after the Napoleonic wars. These wars had been the scourge of Europe, but more a blessing for the neutral US, as WW2 was for neutral Sweden and Switzerland. US foreign trade had reached a peak of $138 m (million) in imports and $108 m in exports in 1807. By 1814 they had sunk to $13 m and $7 m. The US war of 1812 against Canada had at first caused a spurt in US domestic production but faced with a spirited Canadian defence the US finally abandoned the project and domestic industry suffered a decline. Only 4 new cotton factories were established in 1807 but 43 in 1814 and 15 in 1815. The number of banks in the north Atlantic states rose from 25 in 1811 to 111 in 1815. There was a great rise in prices, about 20-30% as the money supply expanded. Competition from European manufacturers increased after the end of the Napoleonic wars and import prices fell in one month in 1815 from an index of 231 to 178. The imports were even sold by auction rather than through suppliers.

Various US banks were issuing their own notes not backed by any tangible resources such as gold or specie (coins). The number of banks increased to 392 in 1818. Kentucky alone chartered 40 new banks in 1817-18. There was considerable land speculation as the country opened up westwards. Imports increasingly exceeded exports. The trade deficit was over $28 m in 1818. Speculators began turning in their bank notes to the banks which exchanged their notes for specie, then the speculators with the specie obtained other bank notes at a discount. The major coin circulating in the US, the Spanish silver dollar, began to trade at a premium of 4% by March 1818. Then the Bank of the US (the Central Bank) began importing specie at a heavy price. Next the debt for the Louisiana purchase fell due, most was owed abroad and had to be paid off in specie. The Central Bank is said to have actually precipitated the crisis of 1819 by calling on the state banks to redeem their heavy balances and notes held by the Central Bank. As a result this bank improved its own debt load ($22 m in 1818, $12 m in 1819, $10 m in 1820) at the expense of everyone else. By its contraction policy in 1821 it held specie of $8 m.

The state banks in debt to the Central Bank had to call in their loans to the public and reduce their notes. About $68 m in

1816 was about $45 m in 1820. There was a wave of bankruptcies throughout the country and a great scramble for a cash position. Inventories of goods were sold off at sacrifice prices. Real estate values and rents dropped. The index of staples fell from 169 in 1818 to 77 in 1819. Land sales dropped from 13.6 m to $1.3 m in 1821. There was large scale unemployment. In the Philadelphia manufacturing sector employment dropped from 9700 in 1815 to 2100 in 1819. In 1820 the secretary to the governor of Ohio wrote "the greatest part of our mercantile citizens are in a state of bankruptcy - the citizens of every class are uniformly delinquent in discharging even the most trifling of debts ."

But although the conditions seemed to be there, this is not what happened in Canada in 1958. Instead of prices dropping or collapsing to clear inventories, prices held firm and credit expanded. At first it was by independent organizations such as Diners Club and a number of small loan companies. As they ran out of funds interest rates for loans increased. The usual 1/3 down on a major purchase became 10% and later 5% or less. Next the chartered banks introduced Visa and Master Card and other financial institutions followed with increased credit creating an enormous expansion. Charges on overdue Visa and other credit accounts rose to almost 20% while the former 3 to 4% interest on bank savings accounts gradually declined to almost nil. This windfall enabled the chartered banks to write down or write off their non-performing loans to third world countries. They also had an opportunity to increase their reserves. By law their loans must be backed by no less than 12% in reserves. This means an increase in reserves of $12,000 paves the way for customer loan increases by another $100,000. The respite from falling prices enabled manufacturers and distributors to introduce 'just in time' inventory and 'critical path' systems to prevent another massive inventory build up.

The lesson from all this seems to be that movement of the economy is unpredictable and one should be wary of financial analysts and economists once they stop analyzing the past and begin to try to predict the future.

We began by asking what effect government economic policies have on the life cycle of societies. I think we can see that today government power has spread across the whole of each modern society, whatever the political system it operates by. The remarkable rapid rise of Nazi Germany after an economic collapse shows that subsequent to an economic downfall the resilience of the society is still there and ready to resume its interrupted existence depending on which phase of its life cycle it may be in.

It also seems that economic revolution is a forerunner of political revolution. Economic revolution causes great misery and some financial ruin, but there is bloodshed as well in political revolution, as in the French revolution of 1789, the Russian Bolshevist 'pograms' in the post 1917 revolutionary period, and the Nazi 'final solution' in the early 1940s.

I think perhaps the most important conclusion is that external sanctions or internal hyperinflation or national bankruptcies of governments or a government stop of currency payments, or a government going off the gold standard, or financial collapses of banks or other financial institutions, businesses or individuals, none of these economic changes in themselves cause the death of a society, although they may involve a transition from one phase to another.

. . . .

We may have found the economy is the lifeblood of a society, but lifeblood isn't the intelligent driving force. That's mind or spirit. We need the equivalent of mind or spirit for a society and its civilization. And that's what we'll look into in our next chapter.

CHAPTER 13
IDEAS

We've found that neither war nor economic factors of themselves motivate a society. They are merely expressions of its behaviour. So what motivates this behaviour? There must be some kind of mind or spirit of a society driving it, within its civilization, and that's what we're going to look into now.

SOCIETIES ARE VARIOUSLY GIFTED

Each society has unique practical ideas to contribute to its civilization. In transportation technology, Britain provided the railway; the US gave us mass use of the car and plane; Germany, space rocketry. Each of these inventions has changed the face of the world.

Within a civilization societies are very imitative. No society can maintain a technological advantage for very long. Nuclear bomb knowhow has quickly proliferated.

THE 'AGES' OF CIVILIZATIONS

Civilizations go through Ages, by which we mean all the societies in a civilization go through the same age more or less at the same time, each in their own way. Our Western civilization has now moved from the Industrial Age into the Space Age, and was previously in the Protestant Age and before that in the Feudal Age. It began in what I call the Unstructured Age. That Age was a ferment of the few remains of Roman society taken over by the Franks, Goths, Longobards, Vandals, and so on. Each Age solves the problems arising in its societies in a different way. These different ways of doing things develop into mind sets which are characteristic of the Age.

The Space Age is based on collectivism, science, electric power and computer and information technology. The more advanced it becomes, the more vulnerable it is to attack and destruction. For example, in warfare today, highly sophisticated and expensive equipment - say a navy frigate - can be destroyed by one missile. A tank or an aircraft can be demolished by a single small missile from a hand-held launcher.

The Feudal Age was far less wealthy than ours, an agrarian system based on land tenure and service with serfs 'attached' to the land. The Industrial Age was based on machinery, rents and wage earners. It arose through a new mind set created by a new belief - Protestantism - aided by the plague of the Black Death which broke the back of the land service tenure system through loss of serfs, and caused service to be increasingly commuted to rents, and the change from manuscript copying to printing of books.

Education in the Feudal Age was inexpensive, for example by the apprenticeship system within guilds or in monasteries. Great cathedrals and universities were constructed during the Feudal Age, so it would not be entirely true to say that education and culture were then at a very low ebb. But education in Canada today is typically taking about 2/3 of total revenue at the local government level and an additional 17% of total revenue at the provincial level. Yet the literacy rates and population percentage of trained professionals in Western societies including Canada, have fallen below the level for some Pacific rim states.

A new civilization, or even a new Age in the present Western civilization, with a different mind set may have a quite different way of inculcating it in its citizens than by schools and universities.

Punishment for criminals was very public and inexpensive in the Feudal Age. Those convicted of minor offences generally had hands and feet locked into 'stocks' on the streets and were usually spat upon or had rotten eggs or fruit thrown at them. Some more serious crimes resulted in branding or loss of a limb. The crimes deemed most serious, for example heresy against the Church, resulted in burning at a stake or beheading in a public place, or being hung, drawn and quartered. Today jailed inmates have access to radio, TV and movies and occasionally wreck the facilities. By 1998 costs were over $50,000 US a year for each inmate, and the judicial system is becoming a revolving door back to society again.

Policing in the Feudal Age was by restricting the movement of people to their own area and making 1 man in 10 responsible for conduct. The 'hundreds' reported to the shire reeve or sheriff. The policing for the Economic Summit of 7 world leaders in Toronto, Canada, in June 1988, a 3 day conference, cost over $5 million, 5,000 media people are said to have come to the city for the occasion. Total local cost of the event was reported as $20 million. Less wealthy societies solve these problems with different ideas in less expensive ways.

THE RISE OF NEW IDEAS
There are ideas not related to technology. These promote fundamental change and underlie the behaviour of the society towards its individuals. My own conclusion is that the rise of an idea to prominence in a society takes about 70 - 90- years as a ½ cycle to dominance, then another 70 - 90 years for decline, a total significant influence of about 140 - 180 years. Ideas that have longer spans are reinterpreted and become quite different afer each 140 - 180 year cycle. This cycling effect seems to tie in with changes from one generation to the next.

One form of fundamental idea is belief; an idea incapable of logical proof. I include ideologies and religions under this heading. Beliefs are usually held dogmatically, are fought over viciously, and can become decadent. Some of the most brutal wars in history have been fought over beliefs: the Crusades, the 30 year's war in Europe, the conquest of indigenous peoples in central and south America, the wars in and around Palestine. Some of the most vicious internal persecutions and struggles in societies have involved beliefs: the Inquisition, the massacre of the Hugenots, the fighting between Catholics and Protestants in Northern Ireland; differences in belief about slavery were involved in the American civil war.

An original thought has a life cycle and by diffusion is simplified into a shadow of its former self. I think today's ideas and beliefs are based on four main concepts:

1.Marxism (1848) is thought to have said that capitalism is evil and must go; the workers should have control; the government should pay for everything.

2.Darwinism (1859) is seen as the survival of the fittest and man evolving in nature as part of the animal world so that a Creator God is not necessary.

3.Freudian psychoanalysis (1900) has become permissiveness. We mustn't interfere with the behaviour of a child or we may adversely affect its development and create in it an emotional block. We mustn't be too hard on criminals, but must try to understand how they came to be what they are.

4.Einstein's theory of relativity (1905) is reduced to the idea that everything is relative, there are no more absolutes. This, combined with Darwinism is leading to the virtual discontinuance of belief in religion in our Western societies.

These are all travesties of the original work of these men. For example, Marx. I think he was, as we all are, a product of his Age, drawing ideas from Rousseau, Paine, Hegel, the French and American revolutions and the then new economic discipline of Adam Smith. What Marx saw, and Charles

Dickens saw, was the appalling fact of 8 to 10 year old children working 10 hour days in factories and mines earning a pitiful income. Sometimes their parents were unable to find work. Marx, by the power of his thought in social philosophy, politics and economics, devised a new system. Basically Marx saw that the people who owned the factories and mines were causing the misery of these poor children and their parents. Therefore, if only the people who worked in the factories and mines could themselves control their workplaces the problem would be solved. Marx carried his thinking to a logical conclusion. Here are some direct quotes from the Communist Manifesto (1848):

"The history of all hitherto existing society is the history of class struggle"

"The modern bourgeois society that has sprouted from the ruins of feudal society has not done away with class antagonism... more and more two great hostile camps... bourgeoisie and proletariat."

"The bourgeoisie has torn away from the family its sentimental veil and has reduced the family relation to a mere money relation"

"The bourgeoisie compels all nations on pain of extinction, to adopt the bourgeois mode of production"

"Owing to the extensive use of machinery and to division of labour, the work of the proletarians has lost all individual character... Masses of labourers, crowded into the factory, are organized like soldiers ... not only are they slaves of the bourgeois class, and of the bourgeois state, they are daily and hourly enslaved by the machine..."

"No sooner is the exploitation of the labourer by the manufacturer, so far at an end, that he receives his wages in cash, than he is set upon by the other portions of the bourgeoisie, the landlord, the shopkeeper, the pawnbroker."

"The proletarian is without property, his relation to his wife and children has no longer anything in common with the bourgeois family relations..."

"The immediate aim of the Communists is ... overthrow of the bourgeois supremacy, conquest of political power by the proletariat "

"The French Revolution, for example, abolished feudal property in favour of bourgeois property. The distinguishing feature of Communism is not the abolition of property generally, but the abolition of bourgeois property. But modern bourgeois private property is the final and most complete expression of the system of producing and appropriating products that is based on class antagonisms, on the exploitation of the many by the few. In this sense, the theory of the Communists may be summed up in the single sentence. Abolition of private property."

"Abolition of the family! Even the most radical flare up at this infamous proposal of the Communists. On what foundation is the present family, the bourgeois family, based? On capital, on private gain... But this state of things finds its complement in the practical absence of the family among the proletarians, and in public prostitution."

"The bourgeois claptrap about the family and education, about the hallowed correlation of parent and child, becomes all the more disgusting, the more, by the action of modern industry, all family ties among the proletarians are torn asunder, and their children transformed into simple articles of commerce and instruments of labour."

" 'But you Communists would introduce community of women', scream the whole bourgeois in chorus. Our bourgeois, not content with having wives and daughters of their proletarians at their disposal, not to speak of common prostitutes, take the greatest pleasure in seducing each others wives. Bourgeois marriage is in reality a system of wives in common, and thus, at the most, what the Communists might possibly be reproached with is that they desire to introduce, in substitution for a hypocritically concealed, an openly legalized community of women."

"Working men of all countries, unite!"

If Marx were set down on earth today he would not be concerned with the working conditions of industrial workers in Western societies, a former problem which is largely solved. Presumably some other great social injustice would concern him.

Ideas cannot be confined within a society. The spread of the ideas of Karl Marx is an excellent example of ideas being seized by a competing society. Karl Marx was the son of a Jewish lawyer in Prussia, Germany, who with his entire family had become a Protestant. Karl Marx studied in the British Museum, and is buried in Highgate cemetery, in London, England. But his ideas did not establish power in either Germany or England. They came to power in Russia and China. Unfortunately he wrote in a spirit of confrontation and violence. This attribute was carried forward into the subsequent development of his views in societies.

What new ideas do we have since the time of those 4 men, Marx, Darwin, Freud and Einstein? Nothing very encouraging. For one, the Principle of Uncertainty. For another, the Big Bang theory. A world of political activism, international terrorism, ruthless religious fundamentalism and nuclear weapons seems to point more to anarchy and a dark age than to a golden age. In the last 70 to 90 years we have made great advances in science and technology, but not I think in the beliefs we live by, except our belief in science itself.

CIVILIZATION AND BELIEFS
Societies are continually evolving new ideas and ways to do things. As a society grows old more and more abstract ideas and ways of doing things have been thought of and led on from one another in a sequence until the possibilities of new approaches become more limited and ways to innovate are more extreme and bizarre. Constructive impetus is lost because no new useful ways are found to develop. That's when decadence sets in.

DECADENCE
Here's an example of how decadence seems to take root and grow in a society:

A telephone company employee was fired for alcoholism, being frequently drunk on the job. This dismissal was after remedial courses were paid for by the company and abandoned by the employee. He took his case to the local Labour Relations Board. As it is not a court but a tribunal, it can dispense with the common law rules of evidence, and has the power to enforce its decisions. In this case it ordered the employer to re-hire the worker and pay back wages for the entire period since he was fired. The company in its defence said that this man's work consisted of going into peoples' homes for equipment maintenance and it did not think it was right that the company should send an alcoholic into peoples' homes. The board thought this was not an adequate reason to deprive the man of his employment.

What interests me in this case is that the rights of the people into whose homes this man would now be going were not considered. Nor was the right of the company to maintain its standards and hire and fire people as it deemed in its best interests to maintain its service. Nor was the fact considered that if a person is not suited to employment in one company or business he or she has the right to go elsewhere and find more congenial employment. But the principles of this generation placed the rights of an individual who is detrimental to the society as taking precedence over the rights of those who are being more constructive in the society. I would suggest that this type of approach, this idea, this belief, goes back fundamentally to the current interpretation of the teachings of Freud and to some extent of Marx. Such a decision has a ripple effect on a society. That corporation will have to take this outcome into account in planning future policy. The tribunal decisions are widely published. Other corporations and business entities will have to take cognizance of this decision. I think it also shows a decline in the survival capacity of the society because there are always young aggressive societies 'out there' with command structures based on merit, prepared to overrun lethargic neighbours. Eventually this becomes part of the winding down of a society, it loses momentum, bogged down by the weight of its increasingly inefficient and impractical interpretation of ideas, and decadent interpretations of its beliefs.

That is why we found the colonization attempts of societies in the ascending or expansionist phase are likely to succeed and those of older societies are likely to fail, because the ideology behind them is in decline. We've also found that wars and economic dysfunctions don't terminate societies unless they're in the final stages of decay. What our test case of Venice seems to show is that when a society is unable to adjust to a changing environment by creating new solutions, but has wealth, it becomes an artistic paradise, then becomes introspective and decadent, loses touch with reality because it can no longer cope with its problems, and deteriorates until it is swept away by rising new societies. When there are no more rising societies to do that, and the entire spectrum of the civilization is in the inert condition, the civilization itself comes to an end and dies.

Next we will apply the theory to two contemporary societies that present some difficulties: Germany and Russia.

CHAPTER 14

APPLYING THE THEORY:
GERMANY AND RUSSIA

In chapter 5 we said Germany began with the Treaty of Verdun in 843 but was a difficult society to interpret. The formative and ascendancy periods end I suggest at about 1231 when Frederick II was Holy Roman Emperor, king of Germany, Sicily, Lombardy, Burgundy , and Jerusalem. But in 1231 the Privilege of Worms gave the various princes in Germany full rights of jurisdiction over their lands and they became practically independent rulers, while Denmark and Poland ceased to be vassal states. So, 843 to 1231 = 388 years, the formative and ascendency phases for Germany.

To judge by our study of Venice and Rome, next should come phase 3, the phase of expansion. What happened instead was that the 'Privilege' of 1231 caused a backward step and Germany degenerated it's said, into over 1,000 little principalities, though some larger ones remained. There's the complication of the Holy Roman Empire, discussed in chapter 5. That began with Otto the Great, a Saxon, chosen as a German king in 936. He was by far the greatest ruler in Europe in his day and in 962 was crowned by the Pope as Holy Roman Emperor. This title went with Germany until 1254. But by 1373 Charles of Moravia was Holy Roman Emperor, king of Germany, of Lombardy, of Burgundy, of Bohemia, which he enlarged, his son received Brandenburg, and he bought part of the upper Palatinate. So there was expansion for the first 140 years of Germany's phase 3.

The trouble with the German society is that it didn't go through what our theory would expect, expansion for up to 300 years or so after 1231. Instead it went through religious torment. John Huss of Bohemia was burned at the stake as a heretic in 1415 but Hussites won pitched battles in Germany until 1434. In 1517 Martin Luther nailed his 95 theses to a church door at

Wittenberg, in Brandenburg, which later became the core of Prussia, in north Germany. Civil wars followed, knights and peasants were in revolt, and all through Germany people were declaring for Luther or the Pope. The mostly northern Protestants were just not going to be forced to become Catholics by the (mostly southern) Catholics, represented chiefly by Austria, then the leader of the Holy Roman Empire. Religious conflict and unrest went on intermittently until in 1618 the 30 years war broke out in Germany. By the end of this war 5 million Germans are said to have died and the population was reduced to 25 million. What happened in Germany is a sad commentary on the effects of beliefs on societies. Germany was devastated. Many villages were totally deserted, agriculture was almost at a standstill, large numbers of land workers had been killed or taken into various armies. Much livestock was destroyed, houses were burned down, industry and commerce had been ruined by the war. There was great inflation in Germany.

But in 1663 the Reichstag had been established in Regensburg. It included representatives of the 8 electors of the empire who were 3 German archbishops plus Bohemia, Saxony, Bavaria, Brandenberg, and the Palatinate of the Rhine. Later, Hanover was added. That was the first house. The second house of representatives came from the various princes, and the third house from the various free cities. So between 1231 and 1648 = 417 years, Germany had made good expansionist progress during the first 140 years or so, but then literally tore itself apart.

Does this mean Germany ceased to exist as a society? I think not for 2 reasons. First, it was Germans fighting Germans, although others joined in; it was civil war, which has occurred in almost every society, including the US, France, Britain, and Rome, without causing the death of a society. Secondly, the Holy Roman Empire existed throughout these troubles and was a German entity under Austria at the time. So the German period which we would expect to be expansionary, 1231 to 1648, was in fact a period under Austrian domination, but with religious civil wars dividing the German people.

In the next phase, phase 4 of this society, we should expect what we have called the phase of dominance, following on from expansion. But as we find that the expansion was cut short it is interesting to see what effect this stunted growth had on the next phase.

What happened was that instead of expansion continuing, the society was thrown back to the ascendancy phase again, and from 1648 to 1866 we see the rise of Brandenburg to become Prussia, to head a league of smaller German states, to survive, as did Austria, the Napoleonic period (which was fatal to Venice), and in 1866 Prussia defeated Austria and finally excluded it from Germany. The result seems to have been that Germany lost about 300 years. This can be seen from the extensive colonization around the world by Spain, Portugal, France, Britain, and the Netherlands, but not Germany, prior to the 1800s.

The expansionary phase resumed for Germany between 1866 and 1914. Prussia not only expanded locally to absorb the other German states except Austria, but having defeated the French society in a war in 1871, king William of Prussia had himself proclaimed German Emperor at Versailles near Paris in France after the victory. Between 1871 and 1914 Germany acquired an overseas empire in Africa, New Guinea, the Marshall Islands, Melanesia, and Kiao Chow in China. By 1907 the population of German colonies was about 12 million, the Kiel canal was built so that German ships could pass between the Baltic and North Sea, and Germany was building battleships twice as fast as Britain which at that time had the largest navy in the world.

So we can say for the period from 1648 to 1914 Germany had caught up into its expansionary phase (the 3rd phase) and by 1939 had entered its 4th phase, of dominance in which it was stopped short militarily by 1945. Since then it has continued by economic expansion and in the 21st century is the major force in the new European Union.

. . . .

Now we should look at the other problematic society on our list, Russia. We found in chapter 5 that Russia had its beginning in Novgorod in 862, controlled by Norsemen. These two peoples, Norse and Slavs were never directly within the ambit of Rome society as were all the Mediterranean rim societies and England. So the beginnings were different.

Kiev developed as a trading centre with Byzantium, and there was rivalry between Kiev, Novgorod and later Moscow, mentioned as early as 1117. But in 1240 Kiev was sacked by the 'Golden Horde' of Ghengis Khan, the Mongols. Later they sacked Moscow. They dominated the area and exacted tribute from 1240 to 1480. Ivan III (the Great) took over Novgorod in 1471 and then threw off the control of the Golden Horde. Russian frontiers were extended to the gulf of Finland and the Crimea. The territory was systematically organized.

The first phases for Russia, then, the formative and ascendancy phases, ran from about 862 to about 1471 = 609 years. This is a longer than average period, probably for two main reasons. First, that Russia is a vast country, which may slow the pace, and next, there was foreign ownership for about 240 years which apparently delayed the process. This delay was probably also responsible for holding the Russian society in the feudal age longer than the European societies further west. It was not until 1861 that feudal serfdom was abolished, making the serfs free men no longer 'bound' to the soil or having to work for the nobles. The French Revolution of 1789 had swept away feudalism in France. In Britain the peasants revolt in 1381 (after the plague of the Black Death) had broken the back of feudalism in Britain; feudal 'incidents' had been abolished by statute in 1660.

We would expect phase 3, the expansion phase, to follow, and it does. I would see this phase as running from about 1471 to 1867 = 396 years. In that time Russia took over parts of Finland, the whole of Estonia, had such organizing rulers as Peter the Great and Catherine the Great. Russia took part in the partition of Poland, and in the third one Poland disappeared altogether. Russia fought back the Turks, defeated Napoleon in their war of 1812. Moscow surrendered and Napoleon entered it but the inhabitants burned it. During its retreat in winter Napoleon's Grand Army was nearly annihilated. By 1814 the Russian armies were almost at the walls of Paris. By 1860 Russia had expanded eastward as far as Vladivostok, had secured part of the coast of Manchuria, and Russian authority reached as far as Korea. Russia now had 1/6 of the world's land surface. In 1867 Russia sold Alaska, not on its continent, to the US for $7.2 million.

Somewhere between 1867 and 1905, or even 1917, Russia changed into its 4th phase, which I have called the phase of dominance. So far Russia has achieved this in three main ways. By 1988, some 70 to 110 years into this phase Russia had established client states in the whole of eastern Europe by military means, and by ideological means into parts of the Caribbean, South America, Africa, the Near and Far East. It was the first society to send a man into 'space' and had in 1988 ten times the space satellite program of the US and was one of the two greatest military powers on this planet. All this despite having lost about 20 million of its people to invasion by the Germans in WW2. In that war the US homeland was neither bombed nor invaded.

The reforms of Soviet Secretary Mikhail Gorbachev came about 140 years after the Communist Manifesto of 1848 and 70 years after the Russian Bolshevik revolution, which fits well with the patterns we are describing. The subsequent collapse of the USSR is also interesting to us because it was precipitated by a crowd of 100,000 at Leipzig, in the part of Germany under USSR control. The crowd systematically destroyed the files and records of the secret police, and in effect told their Russian masters that they had had enough, and this was the end of being shot at for trying to escape over the Berlin wall to west Germany, and being regimented in poverty and suppression in the name of Communism and the teachings of Karl Marx.

Russia now has a temporary setback, because its ideological system did not work well, and did not provide a more utopian society as expected. It is now in the process of rebuilding and restructuring its economy and political system of operating. Because it went straight from serfdom and Czarist dictatorship to Communism, Russia society only had its first democratic experience beginning after the collapse of the USSR, 200 years later than France, and 300 years later than Britain. The example of 19th century Germany suggests that it will attempt to catch up at a frantic pace once its internal stability and a new system of ideas have been established.

The important concept we are trying to understand here is how to recognize the different phases societies go through, how they are driven to express themselves in the process, and how other societies, their contemporaries, can find acceptable ways for them to adjust their relationships with one another so that violence, bloodshed, war, and devastation can be avoided or kept to a minimum.

It was thought necessary to comment on these two more difficult cases to verify that they did in some way conform to the general pattern of societal development and decline being outlined. It is not proposed to go around the various other existing societies in the world to analyze their situations based on the interpretations already discussed. Many of them are more straightforward and follow more easily the phases and life cycle we have described and exemplified. This is not meant to be a definitive study. It is meant to be an introduction which others may wish to pursue further. In the final chapter we will look at Western civilization itself and return to the original question: Is our civilization dying?

CHAPTER 15

IS OUR CIVILIZATION DYING?
Let it be clear that I make no attempt to predict the future of societies or civilizations. If experts in stock market trading cannot even predict the next day's rise or fall of the price of stocks and bonds it would be foolish to think one could predict the future of an entire civilization. But we can at least explore some possibilities.

We know that civilizations can and do die. We see their skeletal remains lying broken on the ground in various places around the world. We have a general sense of how long they survived. Thousands of years. The Mediterranean civilization lasted close to 5,000 years and the Stone civilization about 5,000 years before that. Our civilization is close to 2,000 years old, so it has a long way to go yet by these criteria, unless it is snuffed out by an earth crossing asteroid such as Hermes which missed earth by only twice the earth - moon distance. By celestial standards that is very, very close.

But there is a phenomenon going on even beyond the scale of civilizations, and that is the life cycle of the human race. If we look at the phylogeny of various species on a time scale of geologic proportions we see they have a minimal beginning, expand over time, have a dominant position on earth, and then shrink back to next to nothing again or die out completely. These species spans are said to be very long indeed. For example:

Labyrinthodonts. . . .About 105 million years to extinction
Dinosaurs. . . . . . . .About 150 million years to extinction
Trilobytes. . . . . . . .About 360 million years to extinction

Yet we're also told that probably over 95% of all species that have existed on this planet are now extinct. Many species have been wiped out by celestial events such as we've just described.

We can notice something similar in the evolving of our present human race which is probably not much over 100,000 years old; about 15 million if you include all the ape-like hominids. If you want to include apes (anthropoids) it's about 52 million years and including monkeys (simians) you could push it back to about 68 million years. Even that is quite short on a phylogenic time scale. We are so different from these hominids, apes and monkeys that there seems to be more to it than natural evolution from them to us (see my The Immortals and From Chimps to Humans?). These other creatures are knowledgeable specialists in the means for survival in a relatively small land area. There is no evidence that any of them, from monkeys to hominids, have ever turned their attention to the sky above. It seems unlikely that even the most sagacious monkey, ape or hominid has ever contemplated voyaging into space which humans seem driven to do. But however old as a species you choose to say we are, there is little doubt that we have now reached our stage of dominance among species on this planet.

Somewhere about the time of the beginning of the first civilization we have identified, the Stone civilization, there must have been some dramatic climate change which caused the end of the last ice age and the rising of sea levels around the world by several hundred feet. At the present time there appears to be no generally accepted scientific explanation for this event. From the re-shaped earth after this catastrophe arose the Stone civilization. Its use of mighty blocks of stone for building purposes may represent a period of time when earthquakes and aftershocks were more frequent and climatic conditions more severe than they are now.

Of more interest to us as individuals is not the life time of the human race, or even Western civilization itself, but the future of the societies we live in, forming our civilization. They have shorter life spans than civilizations, because they all have to live and die within their one civilization and don't all flourish at once. Within our very recent system of societies and civilizations the nature of societies is expanding as Age succeeds Age. A new type of society has come into existence predicated on the nature of the defunct Rome society, the last great society of the previous Mediterranean civilization. This new type of society now in existence is what I would call a Continental Society. The expansion and colonization by these societies has been primarily occupied with consolidating their existing territories across their own continents. Examples are Canada, the US, Russia, China, India, Australia, the European Union. They are so large that they have internal problems with language differences, differences of customs, religions, races, even severe climate differences, all within their own borders.

SOCIETY. . . . . .LAND AREA IN SQUARE MILES

Russia. 6,593,391

Canada. 3,851,809

China. 3,691,502

U.S.A. 3,615,212

Australia. 2,967,909

India. 1,229,215

European Union. . . . . Under 1 million

The first four of these Continental Societies are so huge that by my calculations all the land area of the European Union nations could be placed in just two of ten provinces of Canada (Ontario and Quebec) with about 15,000 square miles to spare.

Another phenomenon is the outcome of the natural tendency of a society to expand beyond its borders. Since this world is now more or less filled up with people, and there is an inherent urge to expand, Russia, the US and the European Union, with some assistance from Japan, are sending out robotic space probes and have established human presence in earth orbiting satellites and way stations, plus a US human visit to the nearest planetary body, earth's moon. Numerous unmanned satellites orbit the earth for various purposes.

Psychologically, Western civilization societies have prepared themselves for space travel and what may be found beyond this planet. TV programs such as the original Star Trek and its various successors and Space films have explored endless possibilities of space travel and exploration. For this to happen it will be necessary to break the 'light barrier' just as the 'sound barrier' was broken in the 20th century with aircraft that can now travel at 6 times the speed of sound. Western civilization in its next Age may come to know the solar system as a previous (Protestant) Age did the planet's continents and oceans.

With reasonable human care our Western civilization should have several thousand years to go yet, barring climatic or celestial accidents. Whether or not our civilization is dying is not a problem. It will die eventually, as all life dies, including every one of us. The Mediterranean civilization was not founded by Rome, its last great society. As far as we know the first were the Sumerian and Egyptian societies. Egyptian territory even had three different societies rise and fall during the Mediterranean civilization. The Western societies that rose at the beginning of this present Western civilization will be most unlikely to survive until its end, unless it is cut short by some catastrophe. China may well be the next society to rise to dominance, probably followed by India, then perhaps South America. Australia, and Africa, unless Africa is to be the founding society of the next new civilization. Of serious concern is that we need to understand much more about how the societies in which we exist go through their life cycles within the civilization. We have around us different societies of different ages. For example, we have shown that Germany and Russia are younger in development than France and Britain.

On a small scale we saw Venice fought with Genoa for 150 years, but eventually they were both absorbed in a united Italy. In the same way France and Britain fought in Europe from 1066 to 1815, including a hundred years' war, and fought in and for their colonial empires around the world as well. But from then on all that changed. Both societies are quite elderly and concerned to defend their few remaining possessions and heritage. Britain and France fought together against Russia in the Crimea in the 19th century. They fought together against Germany in WW1 and again in WW2 in the 20th century. Since then they have co-operated to produce a commercial aircraft that is the fastest, most accident free, (and most expensive to travel by) in the world, the Concorde. And they have created a land link by joint effort, the Chunnel. France is already absorbed into the larger European Union and Britain will probably find it necessary to join more explicitly than it has already. France is fighting a rearguard action to protect and preserve its language, while Britain is trying to protect its position as a financial market centre which it does not want to surrender to the Union.

We as individuals live out our microscopic lives within societies and in the process help make them what they are. We tend to think of all the societies living today including our own as contemporaries, but in fact we live in a world and a civilization where societies are as varied in age as a family with children, parents and grandparents all living together in one house at the same time. The needs of the different age groups of the family of societies living in our Western civilization are quite different. We need better understanding as to what these needs are before we can live together with more security.

In my youth I had always thought of life as proceeding along with effort rewarded with some success and the society around me providing reasonable security and opportunity for progress. Now that I have had considerable life experience, lived in England, the US and Canada, studied various periods in history, societies and civilizations, my message is different.

Most of human life for many people has been a miserable condition. In the short space of 50 years during the second half of the 20th century, without a world war, there were ordinary people trying to live out their lives in Afghanistan, the Kurds in Iraq and Turkey, people in Hungary, Bosnia, Kosovo, Korea, Yucatan, Peru, Bangladesh, Rwanda, Sierra Leone, Sudan, South Africa, Palestine, Kuwait, the Falkland Islands, East Timor, Chechnya, Northern Ireland, Northern Spain, Montserrat, Mozambique, or living near Chernobyl.

Expect poor quality, self-centred, corrupt government, excessive taxation, war, civil commotion, injustice in the courts, greed, selfishness and persecution, economic depressions, epidemics, plagues and incurable diseases, drought, famine, devastating floods, forest fires, tornadoes, earthquakes, tidal waves, volcanic eruptions and the occasional world war. When you find something else, more pleasurable, be thankful and rejoice inwardly. It may not last.

Carthage, which died so young, was to a considerable extent killed off not by the Romans, but by its own religion which became decadent. At first sacrifices of animals were made to the gods, in the usual way for that time. But then the priests began telling the ruling class that greater sacrifices were needed to pacify the gods who had caused defeat in war. So in times of trouble it came about by degrees that eventually the fairest children of the noblest families were deemed most fit for the greatest sacrifices. Gradually the finest stock of leadership in Carthage was destroyed by perversion of its religion. Similar misguided practices may have caused the downfall of Mayan society. I would call this behaviour decadent. We should beware of decadence. Decadence can kill a society by corruption of the principles that made it great.

NOTE 1
Here is an excerpt from The Decline and Fall of the Roman Empire, by Edward Gibbon (1737-1794). It comes from volume III of the 1905 Methuen seven volume edition, pages 429-30. Gibbon tells us that the time is during the 440s AD

and Attila, King of the Huns and a Scourge of God, had increased his tribute from the eastern empire of the Romans at Byzantium (now Istanbul and before that Constantinople). It had been seven hundred pounds of gold annually, now increased to two thousand one hundred, plus the immediate payment of six thousand pounds of gold to defray the expenses or to expiate the guilt of the war. The unfortunate Eastern 'Emperor' more in name than reality, had to agree to this. He sent an embassy several hundred miles to the headquarters of Attila, north of the Danube, and fortunately for us, one of the leaders was the historian Priscus. Here's how Gibbon tells us what happened next:

The historian Priscus, whose embassy is a course of curious instruction, was accosted, in the camp of Attila, by a stranger, who saluted him in the Greek language, but whose dress and figure displayed the appearance of a wealthy Scythian. In the siege of Viminacium, he had lost, according to his own account, his fortune and his liberty; he became the slave of Onegesius; but his faithful services, against the Romans and the Acatzires, had gradually raised him to the rank of the native Huns; to whom he was attached by the domestic pledges of a new wife and several children. The spoils of war had restored and improved his private property; he was admitted to the table of his former lord; and the apostate Greek blessed the hour of his captivity, since it had been the introduction to an happy and independent state; which he held by the honourable tenure of military service.

This reflection naturally produced a dispute on the advantages, and defects, of the Roman government, which was severely arraigned by the apostate, and defended by Priscus in a prolix and feeble declamation. The freedman of Onegesius exposed, in true and lively colours, the vices of a declining empire, of which he had so long been the victim; the cruel absurdity of the Roman princes, unable to protect their subjects against the public enemy, unwilling to trust them with arms for their own defence; the intolerable weight of taxes, rendered still more oppressive by the intricate or arbitrary modes of collection; the obscurity of numerous and contradictory laws; the tedious and expensive forms of judicial proceedings; the partial administration of justice; and the universal corruption, which increased the influence of the rich, and aggravated the misfortunes of the poor.

NOTE 2
The bibliography/reading list comprises over 1,500 books and academic journal articles, not considered appropriate to include here.

END